Contents

The Open University

Block 5
Consumption: innovation for sustainability

Horace Herring

— –

T307 Innovation: designing for a sustainable future

This publication forms part of an Open University course T307 *Innovation: designing for a sustainable future*. Details of this and other Open University courses can be obtained from the Student Registration and Enquiry Service, The Open University, PO Box 197, Milton Keynes, MK7 6BJ, United Kingdom: tel. +44 (0)870 300 60 90, email general-enquiries@open.ac.uk

Alternatively, you may visit the Open University website at http://www.open.ac.uk where you can learn more about the wide range of courses and packs offered at all levels by The Open University.

To purchase a selection of Open University course materials visit http://www.ouw.co.uk, or contact Open University Worldwide, Walton Hall, Milton Keynes MK7 6AA, United Kingdom for a brochure. tel. +44 (0)1908 858793; fax +44 (0)1908 858787; email ouw-customer-services@open.ac.uk

The Open University
Walton Hall, Milton Keynes
MK7 6AA

First published 2006. Second edition 2010.

Edited and designed by the Open University.

Typeset in India by Alden Prepress Services, Chennai.

Printed and bound in the United Kingdom by Martins the Printers Ltd.

ISBN 978 1 8487 3055 7

2.1

MIX
Paper from
responsible sources
FSC® C013254

Introduction

This block addresses the question of whether technical innovation on its own can lead to a sustainable future. Could this future be one in which, for example, the UK achieves its target of a 60 per cent reduction in carbon dioxide emissions by 2050?

Is it possible to limit environmental impacts by producing and consuming more efficiently and responsibly, using green technologies, so that human needs can be met without undermining the ecosystem on which the planet depends?

Can technical innovation and human ingenuity alone help overcome limits to growth, as technological optimists argue they can? If this approach is no longer feasible, as many environmental critics claim, then what are the alternatives?

Is it possible to reduce environmental impact by using less energy and fewer materials, yet still improve the quality of people's lives, which is the sustainable development approach? If so, would this mean people having to consume less and therefore having to change their lifestyles, and what sort of innovations would be required for this downsized lifestyle?

This block looks at the relationship between technical innovation, consumption and the environment, and in particular:

- whether innovation encourages greater consumption and economic growth, with consequent harmful impacts on the environment

- how possible it is to design, produce and consume products with less impact – the sustainable production and consumption approach

- whether green technologies can keep pace with economic growth.

The big question is, can design and innovation save the planet from environmental dangers? If the answer is yes, will it mean designing sustainable lifestyles that use less, or designing products and services that do more with less?

Aims and learning outcomes

Aims

Block 5 aims:

1 To ask whether the development of ecodesigned goods and services will be sufficient to ensure an environmentally sustainable future.

2 To review the debate on sustainable consumption and its implications for consumption.

3 To examine examples of organisations and companies that practise sustainable consumption.

4 To explore the idea that a more radical approach may need to be developed, perhaps involving curbs on consumption and changes in lifestyle.

Learning outcomes

After studying this block and carrying out the associated exercises, you should have achieved the following learning outcomes.

1   Knowledge and understanding

You should be able to:

1.1 Explain the concepts behind sustainable consumption and why it is relevant to global environmental issues.

1.2 Describe the limits of the eco-efficiency approach to sustainability.

1.3 Discuss what motivates consumers and the difficulties involved in changing consumption patterns.

1.4 Explain how sustainable products and services often combine technology approaches and lifestyle approaches to sustainable development.

2   Cognitive skills

You should be able to:

2.1 Critically analyse the various arguments for sustainable development and their consequences for consumption.

2.2 Identify products and services that have an element of sustainable consumption.

3 Key skills

You should be able to:

3.1 Apply the concepts of sustainable consumption to product design and development.

3.2 Relate project work to the general theories and practical lessons from the course as a whole.

4 Practical and professional skills

You should have:

4.1 Gained experience with project work.

International debate

This section looks at how human impacts on the environment are determined by the interplay between economic and population growth and efficiency improvements. Population and economic growth results in a greater consumption of goods and services, which historically has brought more pollution. Technology has been able to reduce some pollution problems, particularly those associated with the impacts of acid gases such as sulphur dioxide and nitrous oxides that are emitted in some industrial processes. However the problems of dispersed greenhouse gases such as carbon dioxide (CO_2), which are associated with global climate change, remain.

Some argue that technology alone cannot provide a solution and the answer is also to reduce or limit the growth in consumption, especially in rich countries. A debate over the merits of technology and consumption as a solution to global environmental problems has dominated international meetings since 1992 and has given rise to the concepts of sustainable consumption.

1.1 Impact equation

Levels of consumption and consequent environmental impacts are dictated by a host of factors: population, economic activity, technology choices, as well as social values and consumption patterns. The relationship between these factors was described by Paul Ehrlich (1968), and an equation can be used to forecast environmental impact.

This equation shows that environmental impact (I) can be predicted by multiplying three variables. The three variables are the size of population (P), the level of affluence (A) and the technological efficiency of resource use (T).

$$I = P \times A \times T$$

However it should be borne in mind that this equation is a crude approximation, and the variables P, A and T are not independent – technology and affluence are closely related, and so are population and affluence. Nevertheless the simplicity of the equation is appealing to environmentalists when forecasting impacts of population and economic growth, and the possibilities of technology to reduce impacts – the so-called Factor 4 or Factor 10 solutions, which you first met in the *Products* block (see Box 1 for definitions).

> ### Box 1 Factor 4 – doubling wealth, halving resource consumption
>
> Factor 4 is a phrase coined by energy and resource efficiency enthusiasts, to describe the possibility of doubling wealth but halving energy and resource use – that is achieving a four-fold increase in energy or resource efficiency, or a 75 per cent reduction in energy or resource intensity (von Weizsäcker et al, 1997). A more extreme version of this idea is Factor 10 – that is achieving a ten-fold increase in energy or resource efficiency, or a 90 per cent reduction in energy or resource intensity.

Many environmentalists argue that current global consumption, or rather excessive and wasteful consumption by affluent communities (Figure 1), cannot be sustained for environmental reasons. The current global population is now six billion, and is projected to reach nine billion by 2050. Furthermore, if the world's current population used energy and resources as intensively as the average citizen of the USA, global usage would increase sixfold (Heap and Kent, 2000, p. 3). According to the impact equation, the combination of 50 per cent population growth and current US standards of living for everyone in the world by 2050 would impose a ninefold strain on the Earth's ability to cope. In other words, six to nine planets would be needed to support the population.

Figure 1   The use of vehicles such as SUVs is one of the reasons for high rates of fuel consumption in the US and developed world Source: Comstock Images/Alamy

One solution advocated is to alter T through improvements in technological efficiency. However even a colossal Factor 10 improvement by 2050 – a 90 per cent reduction in energy and resource consumption – would still leave I, the impact, roughly what it is today.

The problems for the world of population growth have been remarked on since the famous essay by the Reverend Thomas Malthus (1970, first published in 1798), who warned of the dangers of allowing population growth to outstrip food supply. His message became a central feature of mid-twentieth-century conservationists who called for population control policies for poor developing countries – the south. (I will use south and north to refer to developing, poorer countries, and developed, richer countries respectively.) Initially the reason was to avoid famines and later it was for more overt environmental reasons such as to prevent the cutting down of forests, to protect wildlife in game reserves and generally to conserve resources. The role of the rich developed countries – the north – in heavily using natural resources and creating most environmental problems was overlooked and ignored by these conservationists. Nearly 50 per cent of the world's population now lives in urban environments where energy and resource use is generally higher than in rural environments (Figure 2).

Figure 2(a)   Many people in the south live in densely packed housing
Source: John Bower/Alamy

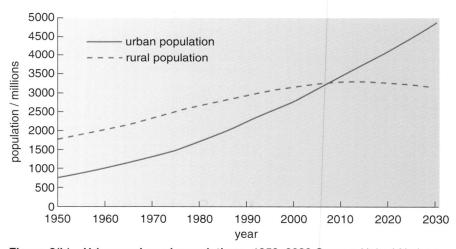

Figure 2(b)   Urban and rural populations, 1950–2030 Source: United Nations, 2004

1.2   Rio conference and sustainable development

In the run-up to and during the first Earth Summit held in Rio de Janeiro in 1992, countries in the north – principally the USA – routinely called for the south to address population growth in order to curb environmental problems. Southern delegates tended to counter this pressure by pointing to consumption patterns in richer countries – consumption that was fiercely defended by the north. It was in the context of this heated debate that the then US president, George Bush senior, made his now-famous remark that 'the American way of life is not negotiable'. In the light of these remarks, the outcome of the Rio debate was almost inevitable. As the south could not agree to curtail population growth and the north could not contemplate curbing consumption, that left the less contentious issue of technological efficiency as the only matter for discussion.

There were angry debates at Rio between the north and the south over which was more damaging: population growth in poor countries or consumption patterns in rich ones. This led to governments adopting the concept of sustainable development. There are many definitions of sustainable development – the classic one often quoted, and which you met in the *Invention and innovation* and *Products* blocks, comes from *Our Common Future*. This document urges that the aim should be to meet 'the needs of the present without compromising the ability of future generations to meet their needs' (World Commission on Environment and Development, 1987, p. 43). Sustainable development is therefore about reconciling two conflicting aspirations – meeting needs and improving the quality of life with the constraint of living within environmental limits and not foreclosing the options for future generations.

Today the discussion around sustainable consumption is changing. Many of the goods consumed in the West are now produced in east Asia and this has sparked an economic boom in countries such as India and China. The distinctions between north and south and east and west are getting blurred and are not always helpful. More people are consuming more products in more places and this is leading to an increasing rate of global environmental change, including global warming, loss of biodiversity and water shortages.

Sustainable development as interpreted by governments is not about reducing levels of consumption, either now or in the future, but about developing strategies that raise standards of living in poor countries and improve the quality of life in rich ones, while reducing waste and environmental damage. This requires a complicated balance to be struck between economic, environmental and social goals. These goals are often referred to as the three pillars of sustainable development.

1.3 Sustainable consumption

Ultimately, sustainable development is about the way goods and services are produced and used by consumers. The main discussion leading up to the Rio Earth Summit was about efficient use of resources from production through to the product life cycle. The main policy document to emerge from the 1992 Earth Summit was Agenda 21, 'an agenda for the 21st century', and it popularised the concept of sustainable consumption.

Agenda 21 had a chapter entitled 'Changing consumption patterns', which said that 'the major cause of the continued deterioration of the global environment is the unsustainable pattern of consumption and production, particularly in industrialized countries' (United Nations

Conference on Environment and Development, 1992, subsection 4.3). Furthermore it called for 'new concepts of wealth and prosperity which allow higher standards of living through changed lifestyles and are less dependent on the Earth's finite resources'. This document provided a potentially far-reaching mandate for examining, questioning and revising consumption patterns and, by implication, consumer behaviours, choices, expectations and lifestyles.

The twin concepts of sustainable production and sustainable consumption were taken up with some enthusiasm by the international policy community, with important reports being produced by the United Nations Commission on Sustainable Development (UNCSD), the United Nations Environment Programme (UNEP) and the Organisation for Economic Co-operation and Development (OECD). They developed these twin concepts into the idea that, by using resources more productively and redesigning production, it is technically possible to deliver the same or equivalent goods and services with lower environmental impact and hopefully social and equity benefits. (This is the resource efficiency model introduced earlier.) These reports have influenced the policy documents of most governments, which have so far placed more emphasis on sustainable production than changes in consumption patterns. As Roger Levett, a leading writer on sustainable consumption remarks, the UK government's main tactic is:

> To encourage competitive markets to bring forward technical innovation to reduce the amount of environmental resources and damage needed to support our comfortable material lifestyles. The two key ideas are 'resource productivity' or 'eco-efficiency' to encapsulate the idea of 'doing more with less'.

(Levett et al, 2003, p. 4)

The World Summit on Sustainable Development (WSSD), held in Johannesburg in 2002, also shied away from issues of lifestyle and consumption, and instead focused firmly on technological improvements in resource productivity and the supply of more eco-efficient products, services and infrastructures. Nevertheless world leaders did publicly declare the need to shift towards sustainable consumption and production, 'delinking economic growth and environmental degradation' (Department for Environment, Food and Rural Affairs, 2003).

decouple
to disconnect two trends so that one no longer depends on the other

The substantial progress made so far in using technology to improve air and water quality despite economic growth has encouraged the UK government to set an ambitious goal to reduce carbon dioxide emissions by 60 per cent by the year 2050. It believes it can decouple carbon dioxide emissions from economic growth if it pursues policies of sustainable production and consumption (Figure 3). For industry the concept of sustainable production, with its emphasis on resource productivity and pollution control, is relatively easy to implement as it fits in well with existing technological methods of production. However implementing sustainable consumption is less easy because the concept is vaguer and less well developed; it is more about social issues of consumption and lifestyle than technologies such as eco-efficiency and clean production.

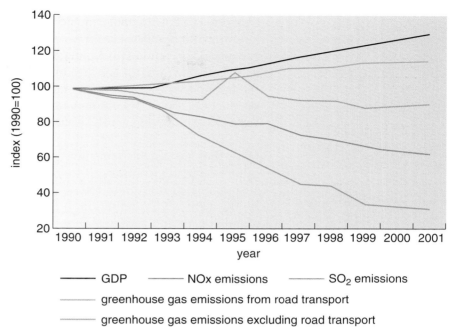

GDP ——— NOx emissions ——— SO₂ emissions
——— greenhouse gas emissions from road transport
——— greenhouse gas emissions excluding road transport

Figure 3 **Decoupling economic growth from environmental impacts, UK, 1990–2001** Source: DTI/Defra, 2003

1.4 Arguing over definitions

A decade of discussion on sustainable consumption has not resulted in any agreement on what sustainable consumption is or should be about. This is reflected in the multiplicity of definitions adopted by various institutions, a few of which are shown in Box 2.

Box 2 Some definitions of sustainable consumption

The use of goods and services that respond to basic needs and bring a better quality of life, while minimising the use of natural resources, toxic materials and emissions of waste and pollutants over the lifecycle, so as not to jeopardise the needs of future generations.

(Oslo Symposium on Sustainable Consumption 1994, quoted in National Consumer Council, 2003, p. 1)

Sustainable consumption is not about consuming less, it is about consuming differently, consuming efficiently, and having an improved quality of life.

(United Nations Environment Programme, 1999, quoted in Jackson and Michaelis, 2003, p. 14)

Sustainable consumption is an umbrella term that brings together a number of key issues, such as meeting needs, enhancing the quality of life, improving resource efficiency, increasing the use of renewable energy sources, minimising waste, taking a life cycle perspective and taking into account the equity dimension. Integrating these component parts is the central question of how to provide the same or better services to meet the basic requirements of life and the aspirations for improvement for both current and future generations, while continually reducing environmental damage and risks to human health.

(Oslo Roundtable on Sustainable Production and Consumption, 1995)

Definitions of sustainable consumption take a variety of views on how much emphasis should be placed on consumers, lifestyles and consumerism. Some are explicit about the activity of consuming and the behaviours of consumers, while others are less clear on the boundaries between sustainable consumption and sustainable production. These definitions also give different emphasis to consuming more efficiently, consuming more responsibly and consuming less. Some definitions ignore these issues entirely. Some insist that sustainable consumption implies consuming less while others assert the contrary. If there is an institutional consensus on sustainable consumption today, it is perhaps most aptly summed up by the 1999 UNEP definition in Box 2: 'sustainable consumption is not about consuming less, it is about consuming differently, consuming efficiently'. As Tim Jackson and Laurie Michaelis, in a report for the Sustainable Development Commission, point out:

> On the question of whether the focus of effort is to be placed on consumer behaviour and lifestyles or on the production of sustainable products, this statement is unhelpfully vague. In relation to the vexed question of whether to consume less or just differently it is uncompromising. Less consumption is not an option. Unfortunately, the combination of these two positions fails to advance the debate over lifestyle and consumerism at all, and leaves government policy-makers most likely to default to a position in which sustainable consumption means simply the consumption of more sustainable products. And the main mechanism for achieving this? The pursuit of resource productivity. Sustainable consumption is equivalent to sustainable production, under this view.
>
> (Jackson and Michaelis, 2003, p. 15)

The UK sustainable development strategy has cast the debate mainly as a matter of consuming more sustainable products, and has prioritised the pursuit of resource productivity in achieving this (Performance and Innovation Unit, 2001; Defra, 2003). As Jackson and Michaelis remark:

> Far from cementing the focus on lifestyle issues inherent in Agenda 21, the WSSD Plan of Implementation ... [focused] firmly on improvements in technology and the supply of more eco-efficient products, services and infrastructures. Once again, these actions are mainly about resource productivity of one kind and another, and typically collapse the distinction between sustainable production and sustainable consumption.
>
> (Jackson and Michaelis, 2003, p. 15)

While there is still debate about the exact meaning and implications of sustainable consumption, researchers all agree it is composed of three elements:

- consuming more efficiently
- consuming differently
- consuming less.

Consuming more efficiently relies on the idea of improving resource productivity or eco-efficiency; examples of this are given in the next section. However, while resources may be used more efficiently, it does not mean that fewer are used, as I will point out in Section 3.

The second plank of sustainable consumption – consuming differently – involves consuming services rather than goods, based on the idea that services consume fewer resources than products. Again the use of services rather than products does not necessarily mean lower use of resources, particularly if it involves higher standards of services or the extensive use of transport or other infrastructure, such as telecommunications networks, to deliver the service. Examples are home deliveries of internet shopping and takeaway meals.

The most contentious aspect of sustainable consumption is consuming less, as it requires an examination of current lifestyles and questioning of consumption patterns. Even if it is acknowledged that quality of life is not really about material consumption, it is hard for most people to give up their possessions, reduce their shopping or cut down their consumption of resources generally. It is always possible to rationalise and give good practical reasons for consumption: a car is necessary because there is no bus to work and it is so much more convenient; you need to fly abroad for holidays because it is cheaper and sunnier than staying at home. Everybody wants to do their bit for the environment but only if it costs little, saves money and is convenient. Efforts by people to consume less voluntarily and adopt more sustainable ways of living are explored in Section 5 in the discussion on downshifting.

The success of sustainable consumption as a political concept has so far rested on the belief that it is easy to consume more efficiently or achieve Factor 4 by using energy and resources more productively. In the next section I look at the widely publicised experiences of some firms that have implemented resource productivity or eco-efficiency.

SAQ 1

Why is the role that consumption plays in causing environmental damage such a contentious issue in international debates?

Key points of Section 1

- Global environmental change (damage) is the result of a growing global population (more P) that is becoming more affluent (more A), in part through increased efficiency of technology (improvements in T).

- Environmental change is the result of increasing consumption by an increasing global population.

- The concept of sustainable development emerged from the 1992 Earth Summit in Rio de Janeiro.

- Sustainable development has in turn been translated into the twin concepts and policies of sustainable production and sustainable consumption.

2 Eco-efficiency

You learned about the eco-efficiency approach to reducing the environmental impacts of production and consumption in the *Products* and *Diffusion* blocks. Here I present some further examples. Case studies show how eco-efficiency has been achieved through consuming more efficiently – both by improving resource efficiency and by altering production processes – and these are followed by examples of eco-efficiency through consuming differently – by providing services rather than products. The section then explores the use of cleaner production methods to eliminate waste products and finally considers reducing the need for materials through dematerialisation.

2.1 More efficient consumption

The first set of case studies shows how ecodesign has apparently produced consumer products with lower energy and material impacts. The second set shows how manufacturers of furniture and electronic goods have designed products that can be more easily recycled or reused, creating less waste and pollution – an important issue given ever more stringent pollution control and waste disposal regulations.

2.1.1 Ecodesign of products

Careful analysis and design can bring environmental and economic benefits to all consumer goods, even the smallest and seemingly most trivial such as matches. The UK company Bryant & May, in its 'Match for the environment' study, posed two questions (Brezet and van Hemel, 1997):

1   How damaging are the materials and processes applied during the production and use of matches?

2   What is the environmental burden of matches compared with other forms of ignition?

With regard to the first question, the ingredients of the match head included three harmful materials – sulphur, zinc oxide and dichromates – while other components such as potassium chlorate and phosphorus were extremely energy-intensive. Finally the packaging, which was responsible for most energy use, consisted of pure wood pulp.

To answer the second question, a comparison was made with disposable and refillable lighters. Clearly a long-lasting refillable lighter is least damaging to the environment because the only thing consumed is lighter fuel, at the rate of 2 grams of butane per 1000 lights. Disposable lighters are the most damaging because they use large amounts of energy-intensive, non-renewable resources, which contaminate the environment for many years after disposal.

Marketing research was carried out to discover how environmental product improvements would be accepted by consumers. These improvements would mean a new match head colour and new packaging. As a result of this study Bryant & May eliminated sulphur, zinc oxide and dichromates from the heads of the matches, made the glue from waste and vegetable starch, the matchsticks from aspen wood from renewable plantations, and used recycled paper board for packaging and materials. To communicate these changes each box carried a brief description highlighting the new environmental benefits (Figure 4a).

Another simple product whose environmental impact has been improved is the Pritt glue stick (Figure 4b). The original design had not been changed substantially for more than 25 years. However, by developing a refillable product, the company reduced the use of plastics by 70 per cent. The designers paid particular attention to achieving a simple design for the refill system and providing refill instructions so that consumers could learn quickly how to fill the Pritt stick.

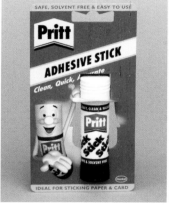

(a)   (b)

Figure 4   (a) Bryant & May matches; (b) Pritt adhesive stick

The most successful designs are those that satisfy the unmet needs of consumers in unexpected ways. For instance in many developing countries many hundreds of millions of people are not connected to the electricity grid and so cannot use electric appliances such as radios or lights.

One solution is electricity from solar photovoltaic cells and another is batteries, but both of these are expensive. An ingenious solution was developed by Trevor Baylis, whom you met in the *Products* block, with his idea of a clockwork wind-up mechanism consisting of a carbon steel spring that drives a generator. Of course the idea of such a mechanism to power products is not new, having been used for hundreds of years to power clocks and toys, and for over a hundred years for such consumer products as the gramophone and the Pianola. As you may remember, Baylis's insight was to use the wind-up mechanism to produce electricity and he developed the clockwork wind-up radio Freeplay, which gives 40 minutes of radio play from 20 seconds of winding. A similar concept is used for wind-up torches. However, Baylis's original design of a clockwork mechanism was abandoned in subsequent models and replaced by a wind-up generator to charge a capacitor or rechargeable battery.

Another consumer product that used long-established technology in a new way was the Greenfreeze fridge, which used the so-called ozone-friendly hydrocarbons butane and propane as refrigerants and in the production of the insulation. Its success depended heavily on the marketing and publicity efforts of Greenpeace to secure advance orders, as discussed in the *Diffusion* block.

2.1.2 Recycling and reuse

Furniture

Manufacturing environment-friendly products is not the end of the story. Disposing of them is an equally important aspect of sustainable consumption. Many items contain toxic elements that cannot simply be thrown away or burnt without risk to the environment. In any case the space available for the disposal of goods is limited and local authorities in the UK are obliged to discourage unnecessary landfill tipping through high landfill taxes.

The Swedish furniture retailer IKEA operates furniture-recycling schemes in some European countries whereby customers return their old IKEA furniture to IKEA stores. Then IKEA's furniture-recycling plants reuse and recycle as many parts and materials as possible. For example, the frame of the Lillskog sofa is made of recycled paper, the Ramp bookcase of recycled aluminium, and the Ogla chair of recycled plastics. Recycled IKEA catalogues are used for the filling in the Ivar doors, and recycled glass bottles are used for the Vanlig handmade glass (Brezet and van Hemel, 1997). Figure 5 shows the Lack table, which is filled with paper and designed to be recyclable.

Figure 5   IKEA's Lack table is designed to be recyclable Source: IKEA Ltd

IKEA not only tries to recycle its old furniture but also encourages customers to extend the life of the product through refurbishment. An example is the Klippan sofa, which has a cloth cover that can be removed for cleaning or repair. IKEA offers new covers to replace old ones when they are worn out or no longer attractive. Consumers can even buy a paper pattern of the cover and other instructions so that they can make new covers themselves.

IKEA's first priority is to reuse as much of the old furniture as possible – it donates reusable furniture to a charity to be sold on the second-hand market. If an item cannot be reused it is disassembled and recycled as far as possible. When recycling is not possible the furniture is incinerated at a power station with energy recovery. Finally, any leftovers are sent to landfills but this volume is kept to an absolute minimum. The few harmful substances that are used in IKEA furniture are treated by a specialised waste-processing company (Brezet and van Hemel, 1997).

An even more ecological approach is taken by the Green Furniture Project in Denmark, whereby at least 80 per cent of the raw materials used in production should be renewable local products such as wood from elms that have died because of Dutch elm disease, ecologically grown flax and waste wool. Traditional bone-based glue is used, together with natural paints and even seaweed collected at the nearby coast, which substitutes for chlorofluorocarbon-inflated foams (Brezet and van Hemel, 1997).

Greener electronic products

Bang & Olufsen is a Danish company producing domestic electronic appliances. In its product design it paid careful attention to energy use, material use and ability to be recycled. For instance the design specification of its portable stereo system Beosound Centur required the stand-by power consumption to be less than 1 watt, whereas typical consumption for an audio system that uses a switched-mode power supply is 5–10 watts. The design solution was to use a more expensive separate transformer, to optimise the chosen components and to focus on only the necessary functions in stand-by – infrared receiver and display. The result was a stand-by consumption of 0.8 watts.

Bang & Olufsen also anticipated European legislation – the Waste Electronic and Electrical Equipment (WEEE) directive, which came into force between 2004 and 2006 (outlined in the *Products* block), required manufacturers to have systems in place to take back and dispose of domestic and electronic appliances. Bang & Olufsen developed recyclable plastic components by the simple measure of leaving them unpainted.

Extending product life

Durability, repairability and upgradability are essential to lessen the environmental impact of consumption. A modular approach allows easy refurbishing and upgrading, and access to individual parts and components, which permits them to be replaced easily. Companies such as Apple (in its computers), Xerox (in its copiers and printers) and Nortel (in telecommunications) have adopted this philosophy. By working to extend useful product life rather than selling the largest possible quantity, companies can squeeze vastly better performance out of the resources embodied in products.

Research results show that reselling or upgrading computers saves 5 to 20 times more energy over the computer's life cycle compared with recycling the materials and components (Kuehr and Williams, 2004). Extending the usable life of computers is therefore effective in reducing all types of environmental impacts. As computers contain many toxic materials, the way they are finally disposed of has a large impact on the environment. At the time of writing (2006) relatively few older personal computers are resold, refurbished or recycled – most are stored in warehouses, basements or cupboards and eventually end up in landfills.

The problem is also exported to developing countries with less stringent environmental regulations. Although some components are recovered, problems such as toxins leaching into the soil are less well regulated. The organisation Greenpeace estimates that 50 to 80 per cent of electronic waste collected for recycling in the USA is exported in this way. Mainland China tried to prevent this trade by banning the import of electronic waste in 2000. However, in 2005 electronic waste was still arriving in Guiya in Guangdong province, the main centre for scrapping electronic waste in China (Figure 6). Greenpeace have also found a growing electronic waste trade problem in India, where 10 000 to 20 000 tonnes of electronic waste is handled each year, 25 per cent of this being computers. Electronic waste scrapyards have been found in Meerut, Ferozabad, Chennai, Bangalore and Mumbai.

(a)   (b)

Figure 6   Many old computers still end up in China: (a) migrant worker stripping wires from computers and other electrical goods that originated in northern countries; (b) workers unpacking a lorry that is filled with computers to be dumped Source: Greenpeace/Natalie Behring

As mentioned above, the European Union has recently passed the WEEE directive to stimulate the recycling of electronic goods, including computers, but the environmental benefits and economic costs depend greatly on how the system is implemented. Recycling managed by a monopolist concern, whose main interest is meeting simple recycling targets for a fixed fee, could result in an expensive system with relatively small environmental benefit. A multilateral concern aimed at maximising reuse across the life cycle of the product presents a more promising picture.

The US computer manufacturer Dell has designed the cabinets of its personal computers to be easily recyclable at no extra cost. The uncoated plastic cabinets can be opened without tools and broken apart with little effort, and have labels that identify the material used, therefore helping recyclers. This desire in the USA for recyclability of computers and other electronic goods is also driven by manufacturers' hopes that their voluntary take-back programmes will avert the possibility of a compulsory take-back law such as the WEEE directive in Europe (Worldwatch Institute, 2004).

Remanufacturing

Remanufacturing involves the extensive reuse of old components, and Xerox – one of the world's largest copier producers – is one of the pioneers of this concept. As early as 1967 Xerox recognised the value of reclaiming and reusing metals from its photoreceptor drums. In 1990 the company embarked on an asset recycling management initiative, which led it to design its products from the beginning with remanufacturing in mind and to make every part reusable or recyclable. This required the creation of an elaborate recycling network, improved materials labelling, and an increase in the use of recycled

open-loop recycling

a product at the end of its useful life is used to make a different type of product

closed-loop recycling

a product at the end of its useful life is used to make the same product again

materials from either open-loop recycling (recycled materials from any source) or closed-loop recycling (from a Xerox source). Xerox's greenest photocopier is the DocuCentre digital series, which is 95 per cent recyclable, is energy efficient, and emits less noise, ozone, heat and dirt than any comparable machine on the market. It is also designed to use 100 per cent recycled paper, which often causes other copiers to jam, and to be serviced by the customer (Hawken et al, 1999, p. 138).

As a result, 70 to 90 per cent by weight of the equipment returned to Xerox at the end of its life can be rebuilt. Like some of its competitors, Xerox also remanufactures spent cartridges for copy machines and printers. In 2001 it rebuilt or recycled about 90 per cent of the seven million cartridges and toner containers returned to it by consumers. All in all, the company estimates that environment-friendly design has kept at least half a million tons of electronic waste out of landfills between 1991 and 2001 (Worldwatch Institute, 2004, p. 108). The remanufacturing process can also be used to reduce waste from other electronic goods, including mobile phones (Figure 7).

Figure 7   Mobile phones being repaired and recycled Source: Topfoto

Remanufacturing logically leads to new ways of thinking about products. Instead of merely selling goods, manufacturers could instead provide a desired service. This leads to the concept of product services or service provision.

2.2   Services not products

As discussed in the *Products* block, the concept of service provision rests on the idea that consumers generally do not want products, they want the services the products provide. They want refrigerators to provide cold drinks, freezers to store perishable food, microwaves to produce hot food, televisions to entertain and cars to transport them to their desired location.

This is the idea behind the product services market: provide the services rather than the product. Simple examples are takeaway foods (hot meals), taxis and hire cars (personal mobility), and launderettes and laundries (clean clothes). In more complex arrangements consumers pay to use products through leasing or renting contracts, rather than buying them outright. By retaining ownership manufacturers also remain responsible for proper upkeep and repair, take the necessary steps to extend product life, and ultimately recover the item's components and materials for recycling, reuse or remanufacturing. Overall the concept has been successful in the chemical industry, has had some success in energy services, and is being promoted in agriculture.

Working directly with customers or relying on retailers, manufacturers can advise consumers on the best lease options available and on the quality and upkeep of products. They can also advise on how to achieve maximum performance with the least amount of energy and materials use, and whether upgrades or other changes would maximise the usefulness of a product. Such arrangements would amount to constructing an entirely new kind of service economy, quite unlike the service economy of today.

2.2.1 Business examples

Have you ever admired the beautiful flower display outside a pub, which looks lovely for much of the year, and wondered how the publican finds the time to garden as well as stock the cellar? The answer is that many pubs buy a hanging basket service from a company whose business it is to take care of the flowers. The pub doesn't need to own the flowers – it just needs the colourful service they provide to attract customers.

Service provision is most developed in businesses where there is a long tradition of contract services and leasing equipment – for instance, Xerox already leases three-quarters of its equipment. Contract energy management, where a specialist firm agrees to provide a business with energy services (electricity and heat) for a set fee, is another example. There is therefore an incentive to produce these services as cheaply as possible through the use of energy-efficient equipment. The US air-conditioning manufacturer Carrier Corporation, instead of selling air-conditioning equipment, is creating a programme to sell so-called cooling services and advising customers on energy-efficiency measures that will help reduce air-conditioning needs.

In the chemical industry, Dow Chemical and Safety-Kleen have begun to lease organic solvents to industrial and commercial customers. Many organic solvents are toxic or flammable or both, and therefore liable to stringent pollution control and safety legislation. The lease arrangement provides customers with a number of legal and economic advantages: safe delivery, removal and disposal, together with advice on proper use and help with recovery, and a strong incentive to use fewer solvents. This system is one viable alternative to the unsafe, polluting methods of waste disposal that are still used in the south (Figure 8). Such methods were once common in the north, but have now been banned.

Another example is Electrolux of Sweden, which offers professional floor-cleaning equipment, medical refrigeration and vending machines on leases, together with a guarantee of quality and reliability. The services are billed monthly as long as the customer needs them. Electrolux therefore has a strong incentive to provide efficient machines, to service and refurbish them regularly, and continually to

Figure 8   Men dumping chemical sludge into a gully in India. Such unsafe disposal methods are now outlawed in northern countries.
Source: Bob Edwards/Science Photo Library

make innovations in its machines and improve its services. As the authors of *Natural Capitalism* comment:

> Electrolux gains competitive advantage in four main ways: providing better equipment, being able to extend its life through optimal use and maintenance, knowing how to package the offer and control its costs, and sharing a diverse fleet of equipment among many users so as to keep it well matched to their changing uses and well occupied overall with a minimum of financial risk. The approach is clearly moving beyond traditional service provisions. Indeed it transcends distinctions between 'products' and 'services', as both 'meld into one to become an offer'.
>
> (Hawken et al, 1999, p. 139)

2.2.2   Interface – a cautionary tale

One of the most unusual and widely publicised leasing arrangements was that conceived by Interface, the world's largest carpet manufacturer. In the mid-1990s Ray Anderson, the founder and CEO of Interface, launched an initiative to slash the firm's environmental impact by leasing, rather than selling, office carpets. In common with other carpet manufacturers, Interface promoted the use of carpet tiles instead of the traditional system of broadloom carpets in offices. Office carpets are usually replaced every 10 years or so when they develop a few worn spots.

In 1995 Interface launched an Evergreen lease under which the company retained ownership of the carpet and remained responsible for keeping it clean in return for a monthly fee. Regular inspections permitted the company to replace only the carpet tiles that showed the most wear and tear, instead of the entire carpet as in the past. This more targeted replacement helped reduce the amount of material required by some 80 per cent. In 1999 the company introduced Solenium, a material that lasts four times longer than traditional carpets, uses up to 40 per cent less raw material and embodied energy, and can be entirely remanufactured into new carpets instead of being thrown away or 'down-cycled' into less valuable products (Figure 9).

However only about a half-dozen or so Evergreen leases were ever actually signed, as most customers opted for a traditional purchase instead. The programme did not succeed for a variety of reasons, some

embodied energy
total amount of energy used in the processing and manufacture of a product

Figure 9 Interface Evergreen leased carpet Source: Interface Europe Ltd

specific to the carpet business. Some customers felt the lease agreement was too complex or too inflexible, locking them into a long-term arrangement that limited their future options. But perhaps the biggest problem was cost – a reflection of Interface's emphasis on high-quality material and high-quality maintenance services. In the end, the company felt compelled to drop the Evergreen lease.

Nevertheless Interface did succeed in substantially reducing its energy and water consumption and cutting its reliance on petroleum-based raw materials (Worldwatch Institute, 2004, p. 110). Interface's strategy for new carpets emerged not from incremental improvement but from a deliberate effort to redesign the flooring business from scratch in order to eliminate all waste and pollution. As Jim Hartzfield of Interface explained to the authors of *Natural Capitalism*, product development began with seeking 'new ways of directly satisfying customers' needs rather than finding new ways of selling what we wanted to make' and 'ecological thinking' led to 'radically expanding the possibilities we found to meet the needs rather than [to] a new list of constraints that narrowed the design or creative space' (Hawken et al, 1999, p. 141).

The Interface story is at once encouraging and cautionary because it is clear the new business model the company was proposing is still facing enormous hurdles. As with all radical challenges to established practice, broad acceptance will not come quickly (Worldwatch Institute, 2004, p. 111).

SAQ 2

List three problems preventing the widespread use of Interface's carpet-leasing scheme.

2.3 Clean production

Subsection 2.1 gave some examples of new products but these can come onto the market only if a manufacturer is prepared to produce them. Production, in turn, has impacts that need to be taken into account. The third plank of sustainable production is therefore clean production, where the emphasis is on the reduction, and perhaps the elimination, of air and water pollution and hazardous waste generation. This requires industry to move from an open-loop to a closed-loop system. In an open-loop system the raw materials are extracted and processed, and substances not directly useful to a factory become unwanted waste, while in a closed-loop system the by-products of one factory become the feedstock of another (Allenby, 2003). This is the basis for the concept of industrial ecology, and a well-known example of this is the Kalundborg industrial park in Denmark (Figure 10).

Figure 10   Kalundborg industrial park in Denmark Source: JW Luftfoto

At Kalundborg one industry's waste product becomes another's feedstock. Natural gas previously flared off by Denmark's largest refinery is used as feedstock in a plasterboard factory, desulphurised fly-ash from the country's largest coal-fired power plant goes to a cement manufacturer, and sludge containing nitrogen and phosphorus from a pharmaceutical plant is used as fertiliser by nearby farms. The present network in Kalundborg evolved over the past three decades from a series of bilateral agreements among a number of local companies, rather than from a master plan. These agreements were concluded in the first place because they were economically attractive rather than because of their environmental advantages (Worldwatch Institute, 2004, p. 103).

So far Kalundborg remains unique as a zero-waste industrial park, but other countries are attempting to build such clean production parks. However, the cleanest production is no production at all and, if the need for materials could be reduced or even eliminated by dematerialisation, that would be a great step forward to sustainability.

2.4   Dematerialisation

Advances in technology and materials science allow many existing industrial processes and products to be redesigned. The weight-performance ratio of construction materials has radically improved in recent decades, enabling the replacement of metals by high-performance composites (Figure 11) and organic conductors, and wood by plastics. Cotton, wool and linen have been replaced by synthetic fibres. Such developments can help conserve both non-renewable minerals and renewable natural resources. However, there are difficulties with these sophisticated materials, alloys and composites, as they can be hard to separate and recycle, and their disposal may involve incineration. Although popular containers such as plastic bottles may be lighter than metal cans or glass bottles, overall their use may be less resource-efficient if they cannot be recycled. However, if collection and recycling schemes are in place, some materials can be successfully recycled into new products (Figure 12).

Figure 11   Mountain bike made from carbon fibre Source: Trek Bikes

Figure 12   Fleece jacket made from recycled polyethylene terephthalate (PET), from fizzy-drink bottles Source: Patagonia Inc.

Supporters of the imminent feasibility of Factor 4 refer to this sort of development as dematerialisation of the economy and hail it as an example of what can be achieved. Careful design has enabled a reduction in the material intensity of the economy, that is, less material is used per euro, pound or dollar of economic output or per person. Furthermore, stimulated by the search for sustainability, there are many exciting innovations on the horizon that may continue this trend: light-emitting diodes, reprintable paper, reusable and compostable plastics, and piezoelectric polymers that can generate electricity from shoe heels or the force of a wave, transforming pressure into electric power.

SAQ 3

Reread Section 2 and list five factors that have influenced designers to produce more environment-friendly products and services. (Other factors that have influenced designers are listed in the *Products* block.)

This section has shown how technological innovation can be focused on finding ways to improve resource efficiency, clean up dirty processes, and reduce or avoid pollution. But can the rate of development of clean green technologies keep pace with the rate of economic growth? Or should the rate of increase in consumption be slowed? In the next section I examine why consumption always seems to outstrip efficiency.

Key points of Section 2

- Some people believe that consumption may be reduced by using green technologies or eco-efficiency: that is, by improving resource productivity – doing more with less.

- Eco-efficiency can be improved firstly by altering production processes, and secondly by providing services rather than products. Finally there are the twin possibilities of cleaner production methods to eliminate waste products, and reducing the need for materials through dematerialisation.

- There are limits to the efficiency improvements that can be made over the life cycle of a product – production, consumption, end-of-life. This is why the continuing drive for sustainability has started to affect the design of new products themselves, as designers think in life cycle or more radical terms.

3 Problems with eco-efficiency

This section explores the relationship between economic growth or consumption and technology or eco-efficiency, and in particular grapples with the question of the rebound effect. This is the extent to which technological improvements or eco-efficiency stimulate economic growth and therefore increase emissions.

In many cases improvements in efficiency are outstripped by an increased volume of consumer purchases. Some innovations, however, are successful in absolutely reducing some pollutants, particularly if they are concentrated at a small number of fixed locations. Examples are sulphur dioxide (SO_2) and nitrogen oxides (NOx) produced during the combustion of fossil fuels in power stations and boilers. For instance, in the UK emissions of sulphur dioxide and nitrogen oxides are down 70 per cent and 40 per cent respectively since 1990. Other pollutants such as greenhouse gases are far more difficult to control as they are produced by millions of mobile sources, for example cars and aircraft, and these have risen despite efficiency improvements (Figure 13).

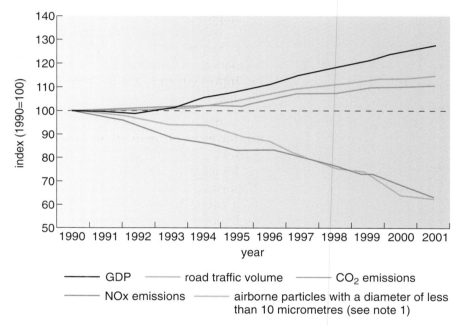

Note 1: PM_{10} particles pose a health risk because they are small enough to penetrate deep into the lungs. The principal source in European cities is road traffic emissions, particularly from diesel vehicles. (Environment Agency, 2006)

Figure 13   Road traffic volume, environmental impacts and GDP
Source: Defra, 2003

A few simple examples may make this issue – and problem – clearer. During the 1990s the fuel efficiency of aircraft improved by about 20 per cent but the use of aviation fuel in the UK rose by two-thirds. The result was greater greenhouse gas emissions despite efficiency improvements. Emissions from aircraft already contribute significantly to climate change, and their contribution is expected to rise substantially in the future because of the increased demand for flights, even though improvements in the technical efficiency of aircraft engines are anticipated. Basically, improved technology cannot keep pace with consumer demand, especially while air fares are cheap and aviation fuel prices low. One solution to reduce demand would be to tax aviation fuel – at the time of writing this fuel is untaxed. Another solution would be to restrict the number of flights by refusing to build new airports. But a cutback in cheap flights would be politically unpopular and the UK government's preferred solution is to build more airports to meet demand.

The road transport situation is similar. There have been improvements in the environmental performance of the average new car – new cars emit less carbon dioxide per unit of power than their predecessors and emissions of nitrogen oxides and particulates are rapidly declining. However, overall carbon dioxide emissions have risen because of a 15 per cent increase in traffic volumes between 1990 and 2001. Cleaner and more efficient engines are being made but people are also driving further in more powerful cars. As Potter and Parkhurst remark:

> Regulation and voluntary agreements have led to improvements in new car fuel economy, but these have made remarkably little difference to the actual 'on the road' fuel economy of the UK car fleet. 'Rebound effects' have emerged, such as changes in drivers' and car buyers' behaviour, compensating for the vehicle improvement.

> (Potter and Parkhurst, 2005, p. 172)

The net effect is that over the past 20 years there has been virtually no improvement in the average fuel economy of cars in the UK or in Europe.

The same is true of domestic appliances: they are getting more efficient but far more of them are in existence, so total energy consumption rises. Between 1970 and 2003, the total amount of electricity consumed by domestic household appliances increased by 123 per cent (Department of Trade and Industry, 2005, p. 106). As Figure 14 shows, the greatest increases in consumption came from the 'brown' and 'cold' appliance groups, although the effect of greater efficiency on the latter can be seen from about 1988 onwards.

Even large increases in efficiency are swamped by growth in ownership: for example, in energy consumption for lighting. Compact fluorescent lighting (CFL) delivers a 75 per cent power saving, yet energy consumption has increased by 50 per cent in the last three decades, largely because of the lifestyle attractions of mood and multiple-point lighting. So it seems improvements in efficiency are often partly or completely cancelled out by the growth in consumption – this phenomenon is known as the rebound effect.

3.1 Rebound effect

The rebound effect or take-back effect is the term used to describe the effect on consumption of an efficiency improvement that, by lowering the cost of producing or operating a product or service, encourages people to use more of it. For instance, when a 75-watt incandescent bulb is replaced by an 18-watt compact fluorescent bulb (Figure 15) – a reduction in power (wattage) of about 75 per cent – over time a 75 per cent energy saving could be expected. However, this is seldom achieved. When consumers realise the light now costs less per hour to

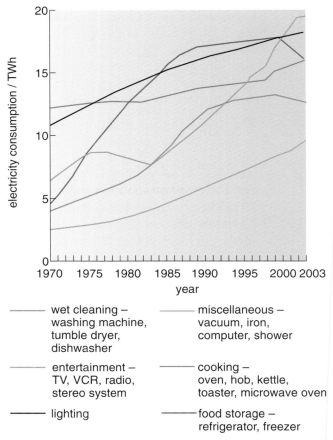

wet cleaning –
washing machine,
tumble dryer,
dishwasher

miscellaneous –
vacuum, iron,
computer, shower

entertainment –
TV, VCR, radio,
stereo system

cooking –
oven, hob, kettle,
toaster, microwave oven

lighting

food storage –
refrigerator, freezer

Figure 14   UK electricity consumption by type of domestic household appliance, 1970–2003 Source: Department of Trade and Industry, 2005

run they are often less concerned about switching it off – indeed they may intentionally leave it on all night. They therefore take back some of the energy savings in the form of higher levels of energy service – more hours of light. This is particularly the case when the user considered the previous level of energy services, for instance heating, to be inadequate. The energy savings from efficiency improvements such as increased levels of insulation may then be spent on much higher heating standards – the consumer benefits by getting a warmer home for the same or lower cost than previously.

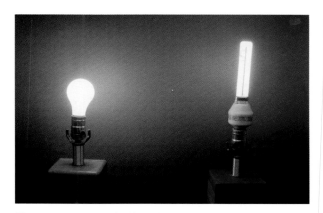

Figure 15   Light bulbs with similar brightness: 75-watt incandescent tungsten bulb (left) and 18-watt compact fluorescent bulb (right) Source: Alamy Images

There are three main types of rebound effect.

1 The *direct rebound* or *price effect* is the increased use of energy services caused by a reduction in the price because of greater efficiency. This works exactly as would the reduction in price of any commodity and has immediate effects.

2 The *secondary* or *income effect* is caused by increased expenditure on other goods and services because of the reduced price of eco-efficient goods and services. For instance, some people might spend the savings from insulating their home on a foreign holiday.

3 The *transformational* or *indirect effect* is the effect of efficiency changes on the direction and pace of technical change and innovation in the economy.

The indirect effect has probably the greatest impact in the long term of all three effects (Herring, 2005). It occurs when new goods and services are created to take account of the possibility of lower energy costs. For instance, innovators and manufacturers, aware that the cost of lighting with CFLs has fallen by 75 per cent, will devise new lamps for new lighting uses – perhaps security or flood lighting or lighting for previously unlit areas such as the garden or patio. The market for lighting therefore increases and total energy consumption soon outstrips the original savings as consumers buy the new lights. Consumers may have energy-efficient lights but they have far more of them and leave them on longer.

A similar effect occurs with domestic energy consumption. Successive UK governments have made improving insulation levels in housing a top priority but, while insulation levels have risen and appliances have become more efficient, total energy use in households has risen too (Figure 16). This is due partly to an increase in the number of households but also to higher heating standards – more widespread central heating systems and higher indoor temperatures – made feasible by improvements in insulation and boiler efficiency. Energy is also so cheap, relative to its cost in the past, that consumers can afford to heat the outside air with patio heaters (Figure 17).

SAQ 4

Name the three components of the rebound effect discussed above, and identify which is most important in the short run and in the long run.

3.2 Factor 10 achievements

The story over the past century has been one of enormous improvements in the efficiency with which energy and materials or resources are used, but there has been an absolute increase in resource consumption (Figure 18). Energy-efficient homes such as those in Figure 19 help to reduce energy consumption but economic growth, caused by the demand for more, higher-quality products and services, has outstripped efficiency gains. So the volume of resources produced and consumed, and hence the total pollution and wastes, has increased. Those industries that have grown the most often show the greatest improvements in efficiency, as can be seen with electricity generation or electric lighting.

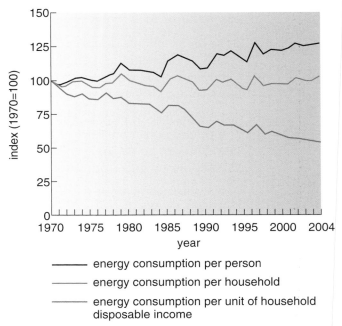

energy consumption per person

energy consumption per household

energy consumption per unit of household disposable income

Figure 16 Trends in UK domestic energy consumption, 1970–2004
Source: Department of Trade and Industry, 2005

Figure 17 Patio heaters raise the outside temperature

One area that has seen vast strides with Factor 10 and more improvement is the decarbonisation of energy sources, which has important implications for the amount of carbon dioxide released into the atmosphere. There is a historic trend towards less carbon-intensive fuels, which have a much lower ratio of carbon (C) to hydrogen (H) in their atomic structure. In the mid-nineteenth century wood was the

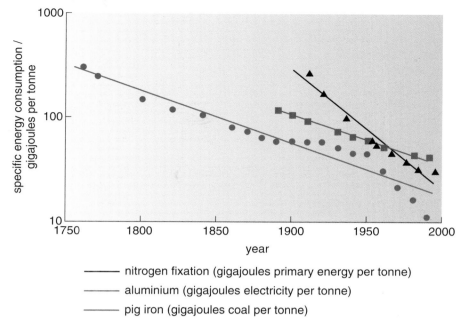

Figure 18   **Specific energy consumption of various materials, 1750–2000**
Source: de Beer, 1998

Figure 19   **BedZED energy-efficient housing**

primary energy source with a C:H ratio of 10; then came coal in the early twentieth century with ratio of 1, followed by oil in the late twentieth century with a ratio of 0.5; oil is now making way for natural gas with a ratio of 0.25. Despite this 40-fold improvement in the C:H ratio, total carbon emissions have risen over 50-fold since the mid-nineteenth century because the world energy consumption has risen 100-fold (Figure 20).

In recent decades legislation, brought about to some extent by environmental activists, has spurred the introduction of pollution control technologies and led to a general reduction in some types of

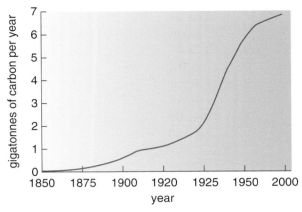

Figure 20 Global carbon emissions, 1850–2000 Source: Smil, 2003

pollution. However, there are some difficult problems related to patterns of consumption, for instance rubbish disposal, carbon emissions, and habitat and biodiversity loss. So although eco-efficiency, backed by legislation and targets, has solved some problems, to expect it to do much better in the future calls for some explanation as to why the future should be markedly different from the past. Why should there suddenly now be a step change in the rate of technical innovation that would lead to actual environmental savings? As Jackson and Michaelis remark:

> ... there is very little evidence to suggest that resource productivity improvements as high as 5–8% per year could be maintained throughout the industrial world over a period of 30–50 years, as required by the Factor 10 goal. From the labour productivity data we can see that it is possible to maintain rates of improvement of 2–3% per year over the long term. But we should bear in mind that labour is the largest single cost in the economy, and both workers and employers have strong incentives to increase its productivity. Massive shifts in policy would be required to provide the incentives needed for sustained resource efficiency improvements.

> (Jackson and Michaelis, 2003, pp. 19–20)

SAQ 5

Name three areas where Factor 10 improvements have been achieved.

3.3 Digital economy

One innovation proposed is that the digital economy – otherwise known as the new, weightless or knowledge economy – will bring forth dematerialisation. However, after the dotcom euphoria of the early 2000s it is not at all clear this innovation will automatically or necessarily be good for the environment. Like the prediction of the paperless office, evidence that the digital economy will lead to dematerialisation does not live up to the propaganda. Indeed, some research shows that information and communication technology can increase consumption, particularly if it stimulates personal travel or freight traffic (Rejeski, 2002). For instance, buying books on the internet can mean they are air-freighted to the purchaser.

The internet can increase the desire for travel and meetings, and has certainly aided the development of low-cost airlines, which has greatly stimulated tourism. Its effect is similar to previous revolutions in communications (newspapers, telegraph, telephone, radio, television) over the last 150 years. The knowledge these technologies bring stimulates transport growth through opening up new commercial possibilities and increasing the desire to travel to new places. The railway developed in tandem with the telegraph, the automobile with the phone, the plane with radio, and now mass global tourism with television and the internet (Figure 21).

(a) (b)

(c)

Figure 21 (a) Steam train and telegraph. (b) 1920s car and phone box. (c) Online flight booking webpage. Sources: (a) NRM/Science and Society Picture Library; (b) Getty Images; (c) www.easyjet.com

The competitive global markets that exist nowadays require firms to make the most efficient use of all their factors of production – capital, labour, resources, and time. This emphasis on what is known as total factor productivity in manufacturing, services and agriculture does not necessarily lead to environmental resource productivity or eco-efficiency. It may be most cost-effective for firms to substitute resources and energy in order to reduce labour costs or to save time. Hence the transfer of manufacturing from northern countries to China, the import of fresh flowers and vegetables by air freight from Africa or South America, the transfer of call centres from the UK to India (Figure 22). The savings in labour and capital costs far outweigh the increase in transport and environmental costs. As Roger Levett remarks:

> As long as environmental resources and impacts are cheap compared to other factors of production such as labour and

capital, companies will concentrate on getting more production out of these other factors even if the methods they adopt to do so add to environmental impacts, as often happens with (for example) mechanisation of manual processes, 'just in time' delivery of components and concentration of distribution in a few centres.

(Levett et al, 2003, p. 7)

Figure 22   (a) Indian call centre. (b) Chinese factory producing car. (c) Transporting flowers by air. Source: (a) and (b) Empics; (c) Photodisc

Despite the dotcom and Factor 4 euphoria, the current situation of relatively cheap energy and resources is moving the world towards greater material consumption, as I have already stated. There are examples of businesses practising eco-efficiency with good results, as you saw in Section 2 and the *Products* block, but it is important not to be lulled into a false sense of security. Levett warns about the so-called Mississippi fallacy, whereby focusing on the few boats struggling upstream results in failure to see the vast body of water pouring downstream. In the context of sustainability, too much concentration on green case studies that are striving for sustainability may lead to the huge problem of unsustainability being ignored. The world is not automatically getting greener. Many of the indicators, especially carbon dioxide emissions, are heading in the wrong direction. However, if energy were to get much more expensive, say oil at over $100 a barrel, then these trends might slow down or even reverse.

3.4   Political critiques

Success in controlling some pollutants through technology has encouraged governments to rely on technological approaches to tackling environmental damage. The UK government is a strong believer in the merits of eco-efficiency, and this can be seen in its reports on sustainable development and resource productivity.

However its approach is criticised by its own advisers, the Sustainable Development Commission (SDC). When the report *Shows Promise: But Must Try Harder* was published in 2004, Jonathan Porritt, chair of the SDC, complained in the press release (13 April 2004) that:

> Far more effort needs to be made to differentiate between 'smart growth' (that generates wealth and social benefits without damaging the environment) and today's wholly unsustainable growth that inevitably ends up damaging people's real quality of life. We must see a more determined effort to reduce greenhouse gas emissions, a move away from consumption as the sole route to wellbeing, and new policies that lead to healthier environments and lifestyles for all.
>
> (Sustainable Development Commission, 2004a, p. 2)

To advocates of sustainable consumption such as Jonathan Porritt, the government is failing to make the tough decisions needed about consumption patterns because politicians and voters are concerned more about the practical realities of their jobs and salaries than about the hazy ideals of sustainable consumption. As a recent report from the Royal Society remarks:

> Unsurprisingly, the concept of sustainable consumption is not popular with governments. It wins few votes and provides an implied threat to competitiveness, employment and profitability. Instead citizens are encouraged to spend, spend and spend.
>
> (Heap and Kent, 2000, p. 1)

A few writers are even more critical, dismissing government statements on sustainable consumption as what they call fashionable greenwash – an attempt to give the appearance to voters of concern about environmental issues while avoiding the difficult realities. At present, 'sustainable' is a popular word to use when referring to new initiatives – for instance, Dongtan city in Shanghai (Figure 23) has been labelled as the world's first sustainable city – but what this actually means is generally left unspecified, and is open to debate. As the Dutch economists Jeroen van den Bergh and Ada Ferrer-i-Carbonell comment:

> Sustainable consumption is a term that follows the popularity of combining a particular word with 'sustainable' ... Examples are sustainable agriculture, sustainable transport, sustainable city, sustainable growth, sustainable population, sustainable tourism and sustainable transport.
>
> (van den Bergh and Ferrer-i-Carbonell, 2000, p. 118)

Van den Bergh and Ferrer-i-Carbonell point out the contradictory nature of such word combinations and argue that sustainable consumption, like sustainable transport or the sustainable city, can be assessed only by a life cycle analysis approach, which can be difficult. However, if the term sustainable is used to mean eco-efficient, less polluting or less resource wasting then it can be assessed much more easily. The current institutional consensus has tended to settle for this eco-efficiency approach, partly because it is – in an age of targets – so much easier to implement, quantify and communicate. But critics argue that it fails to address important questions about the scale of

Figure 23   Dongtan Eco-city in Shanghai is claimed to be the world's first sustainable city Source: Arup

consumption, the nature of consumer behaviour and the relevance of lifestyle change. As Jackson and Michaelis ask:

> So why precisely is the consumption side of the sustainable development debate so contentious? Why has mainstream policy been so reticent to follow up on the Rio commitment to lifestyle change? Is consumption just too hot to handle? Is it too complicated to understand? Or do those in positions of influence simply recognise that it is against their interests to carry the debate forward?

> (Jackson and Michaelis, 2003, p. 16)

These authors believe institutional reticence in addressing these issues hinges on three concerns.

- Dealing with them properly would involve questioning fundamental assumptions about the way modern society functions.

- Any attempt to address consumption challenges people to undergo personal change.

- Questioning consumption threatens a wide variety of interests committed to economic growth – businesses, employees and governments – which makes it hard for there to be any serious discussion about changing or reducing levels of consumption.

Governments, critics believe, are reluctant to interfere with consumer choice and consumer freedom. The implicit assumption is that individuals rather than governments are best placed to decide what are consumers' needs and what are more frivolous wants. At the heart of politics in rich countries is the belief that increased consumption improves the quality of life. It is largely for this reason that economic growth is seen as a worthy objective, as it is assumed to give individuals and society more choice about what is consumed. As social scientists Andrew Jordan and Tim O'Riordan write: 'Today, reducing consumption by some kind of politically inspired intervention or price control is widely regarded as being wholly infeasible by most conventionally minded politicians and is condemned outright as moral dictatorship in some quarters' (2000, p. 94).

These comments about the unwillingness of most politicians to advocate reducing consumption should be seen in the context of the remark by US President George Bush senior that 'the American way of life is not negotiable' (see Section 1) and the fate of an earlier president, Jimmy Carter, who talked about cutting consumption (see Box 3).

Box 3 Carter's calls for restraint

The experience of ex-president Jimmy Carter is burned on the political consciousness not only of politicians in the USA but of those in other countries as well. First, in 1977, he appeared on television wearing a cardigan (Figure 24) and suggested that Americans could save energy by wearing warmer clothes.

Figure 24 During his 1977 speech, president Carter wore a cardigan to demonstrate to Americans the need to save energy Source: Getty Images

Then in 1979, during the second energy crisis, Carter gave a nationally televised speech in which he said the nation was facing a crisis that was the moral equivalent of war. He called on the American public to practise restraint in order to save energy and he said:

> In a nation that was proud of hard work, strong families, close-knit communities, and our faith in God, too many of us now worship self-indulgence and consumption. Human identity is no longer defined by what one does but what one owns ... owning things and consuming things does not satisfy our longing for meaning. We have learned that piling up material goods cannot fill the emptiness of lives which have no confidence or purpose.

> (quoted in Shi, 1985, p. 271)

Instead he preached that people should rediscover the traditional American values of frugality, mutual aid and spirituality – values later to be at the core of the concept of sufficiency. Carter was widely derided for his views and lost the presidency by a landslide to Ronald Reagan in 1980.

With such historical experience, the current debate about consumption in rich countries is framed not in terms of restraint and cutting consumption but in terms of how to redirect consumption. Politicians find it far more attractive to concentrate efforts on production, through eco-efficiency, than to confront the problems of consumption.

While agreeing that eco-efficiency is necessary and to be encouraged, many environmental writers view it as insufficient and call for government action, with social and economic policies for improving the quality of life rather than increasing material consumption. The critics are unclear about what needs to be done. This is a contentious area because it is difficult to reach an agreement about what sustainable consumption is. Nevertheless, all are agreed that science and technology alone will not provide a route towards sustainable consumption. The concept is just too complex. As the Royal Society report says:

> Consumption is at the centre of sustainable development (which everyone seems to want) and one of the great challenges ... must be to make the concept intelligible by a better understanding of the patterns of consumption, what drives them, and how efficiency of consumption can be improved.

> (Heap and Kent, 2000, p. 1)

SAQ 6

What three criticisms have been made of the UK government's approach to sustainability?

The next section attempts to untangle the various meanings of sustainable consumption, investigates what drives consumers to consume, and asks how easy it is to change consumption patterns.

Key points of Section 3

- Promoting eco-efficiency has not yet resulted in lower consumption.

- The rebound effect means that efficiency improvements stimulate consumption, and so the impact of improvements in efficiency is weakened.

- Political critiques of sustainable consumption make the point that efficiency is not enough and instead emphasise the need for less consumption.

4 Understanding consumption

This section summarises the numerous theories of consumer behaviour and the criticisms of consumption from a wide variety of disciplines, and stresses the deep psychological roots the act of consumption has in industrialised society. It also stresses that, to be successful, sustainable design should understand today's lifestyles and engage with the social and psychological objectives of consumers.

Throughout the centuries there has been criticism from religious leaders about the dangers of the love of material possessions or what is now called consumerism or the consumer society. These early moral concerns over adverse effects of consumption upon the individual and society were later joined by environmental ones, which highlight the adverse effects of consumption for the planet. Finally there are the ethical concerns over fair trade issues.

There are therefore three distinct criticisms of current consumption patterns:

- unsustainable environmental pressure and resource depletion

- an alleged failure to contribute to an improvement in human well-being or happiness

- exacerbating inequality and hence fostering social and political tensions.

This triple agenda is noticeable also in the efforts of some businesses to practise corporate social responsibility or producer responsibility or product stewardship: that is, producing goods and services with the minimum of adverse environmental or social impact. Their efforts can be seen in their company reports, which give details of their triple bottom line – an audit of not only their finances but also their environmental and social and/or ethical performance.

To remind yourself of some of these ideas, see the *Products* block video 'Philips: design for sustainability' on the T307 DVD.

4.1 Criticising consumption

4.1.1 Environmental problems

The physical impact of too much consumption is plain to see: gashes in the earth from mining; the cutting down of forests for timber or plantations; waste dumps; and the building of new roads, airports and shopping centres. This physical destruction has long motivated those concerned with the protection and conservation of nature and its flora and fauna, and much has been achieved.

More recent concern is over more invisible threats: acid rain and the ozone hole in the 1980s, and climate change since the 1990s. However, with these complex global and largely invisible problems it is hard to link cause and effect, and definitive answers and solutions may take years, if not decades, to emerge.

Consumers are often aware of these problems but they may lack access to what they consider independent information about the extent of the harm caused by their actions. The public is now less likely to accept scientists or government as authorities on what the problem is and what should be done about it. So action is slow, particularly if it involves public participation, as would be necessary to change patterns of consumption.

A first step is to convince consumers of the adverse consequences of their consumption, some of which are shown in Figure 25. One way this can be done is by ecological footprinting, a technique that essentially accounts for the sustainable use of the planet's energy and resources and demonstrates how changes in consumption could lower pressure on these resources. The ecological footprint of a given population – which could be a household, city, region, country and so on – is determined by calculating the area of land required to support indefinitely the lifestyle of that population. This footprint is then compared with the amount of land needed to support a population consuming the global average. If the given population's footprint is higher than the global average, it might be seen as unsustainable.

(a) (b) (c)

Figure 25 The environmental destruction associated with consumption results in loss of wildlife and human habitats: (a) mining and drilling; (b) felling of the rainforests; (c) disposal of rubbish Sources: (a) Robin Smith/ Photo Library (b) Ecoscene/Sally Morgan, (c) Still Pictures

Table 1 shows the ecological footprint of consumers in some of the larger countries. The greatest ecological footprint is that of the USA, which is over four times the global average. The USA is followed closely by that of Australia at three and a half times the average; the UK's is two and a half times the average, while the footprints of poor countries such as Bangladesh and Ethiopia are less than one-third of the average. So the average consumer in the richest country, the USA, has a global impact nearly 16 times greater than that of the poorest. This supports the arguments made in Section 1 that consumption in the north is currently the main cause of global environmental problems, although the south could quickly catch up and overtake.

Table 1   Ecological footprints

Country	Total ecological footprint (hectares per person)	Population (millions)
Bangladesh	0.6	140.9
Ethiopia	0.7	67.3
India	0.8	1033.4

Country	Total ecological footprint (hectares per person)	Population (millions)
Nigeria	1.2	117.8
China	1.5	1292.6
Egypt	1.5	69.1
Brazil	2.2	174.0
World	**2.2**	**6148.1**
Mexico	2.5	100.5
Italy	3.8	57.5
Japan	4.3	127.3
Russian federation	4.4	144.9
Germany	4.8	82.3
United Kingdom	5.4	59.1
France	5.8	59.6
Australia	7.7	19.4
United States of America	9.5	288.0

Source: World Wide Fund for Nature, 2004

4.1.2 Social effects

Religious leaders, moralists and social and political reformers have for a long time made many criticisms of consumerism. It is accused of corrupting the individual, undermining the community and sapping civic virtues. Instead the simple life of moderation, thrift and self-sufficiency has been praised, although its message has been accepted only under conditions of duress caused by wartime rationing or mass unemployment. Some social critics regard consumerism as the central negative feature of modern industrial societies and as a means of persuading people to passively acquiesce to the given power structure of society.

One critic, Brian Heap, in the Royal Society report, compares the problems of excessive consumption of resources to those posed by the excessive consumption of food, asserting, 'the current epidemic of obesity is caused largely by an environment that promotes high intake through excessive consumption' (Heap and Kent, 2000, p. 1). In both cases, he argues, the solution is reduced consumption and lifestyle changes, and that just as the government has difficulties with tackling obesity, so it will with consumption.

Other social critics accuse consumption not only of ruining people's physical and mental health, but also of causing them to work excessive hours to earn the money to consume. It has been an age-old dream of social reformers that technical progress in production would lead to a shorter working week and more leisure time. Instead the result has been greater consumption. For instance Juliet Schor, a US sociologist, comments: 'liberating society from the toils of labour is an old utopian dream which has been superseded by the ideology of growing consumption in modern industrial societies' (Schor, 1992, quoted in Cogoy, 1999, p. 386).

Despite these criticisms of consumption, the ideology of growing consumption – that more goods are desirable – pervades all political parties and social groups. Even the consumer movement itself campaigns primarily for good-quality consumer products at affordable prices, with some concern over environmental quality and fair trade issues.

4.1.3 Equity

The gap between the rich and the poor in the world is plain to see, and this gap strikes many people as unfair. The wealthiest countries in the north, such as the USA, enjoy consumption levels a hundred times higher than those of the poorest in the south, such as Nigeria (Table 2). Overall one-quarter of the world's population (1.7 billion) enjoy northern standards of living with an income of over $20 a day, while nearly half (2.8 billion) are poor, living on less than $2 a day, and a fifth (1.2 billion) live in extreme poverty on less than $1 a day (Worldwatch Institute, 2004, p. 6).

Table 2   Household consumption in selected countries

Country	Household consumption expenditure (dollars per person per year[1])	Electricity (kilowatt-hours per person per year)	TVs, mobile phones and PCs[2] (per thousand population)
Nigeria	194	81	79
India	294	355	95
Ukraine	558	2293	518
Egypt	1013	976	276
Brazil	2779	1878	591
South Korea	6907	5607	1540
Germany	18580	5963	1703
USA	21707	12331	1911

[1] The dollar value used is 'constant 1995 dollars', which represents a dollar based on a 1995 value and ignores the inflation that can distort purchasing power.
[2] The sum of TVs plus mobile phones plus personal computers.
Source: adapted from Worldwatch Institute, 2004

The impacts of consumption levels in the north are often bigger than the impacts of population growth in the south. The UK population, growing at a rate of about 120 000 people per year, may be growing much more slowly than the 2.4 million per year in Bangladesh, but this annual increase in population in the UK causes more than double the increase in carbon dioxide emissions than the annual population growth in Bangladesh. This is because the per-person consumption level and carbon dioxide emissions are so much higher (over 40-fold) in the UK than in Bangladesh (Heap and Kent, 2000, p. 153). Similarly the population growth of 3 million per year in the USA causes an increase in carbon dioxide emissions three times greater than does the annual 16 million increase in India (Table 3).

Table 3 Energy consumption and carbon dioxide emissions in selected countries

Country	Commercial energy (tonnes of oil equivalent per person per year)	Oil (barrels a day per thousand population)	Electricity (kilowatt-hours per person per year)	Carbon dioxide emissions (tonnes per person per year)
USA	8.1	70.2	12331	19.7
Japan	4.1	42.0	7628	9.1
Germany	4.1	32.5	5963	9.7
Poland	2.4	10.9	2511	8.1
Brazil	1.1	10.5	1878	1.8
China[3]	0.9	4.2	827	2.3
India	0.5	2.0	355	1.1
Ethiopia	0.3	0.3	22	0.1

[3] Excluding Hong Kong
Source: Worldwatch Institute, 2004

The world can be divided into three consumer classes (illustrated in Figure 26):

1 *The rich.* These people have an affluent lifestyle and half of them live in the north, making up over 90 per cent of the northern population. Many of them travel extensively by car and plane; eat high-fat, high-calorie, meat-based diets; drink bottled water; use throwaway products; and live in spacious, climate-controlled houses with many appliances. Their average carbon dioxide emissions are over 10 tonnes per person per year.

2 *Middle income.* About the same in number as the rich, and aspiring to the same lifestyle, these people are mostly concentrated in southern countries but there are pockets of them living in what is called poverty in northern countries. Their annual average emissions of carbon dioxide are about 3 tonnes per person.

3 *The poor.* These people make up about half the world's population. They are just surviving but are vulnerable to natural disasters and the impacts of global warming. Their annual average emissions of carbon dioxide are lower than 1 tonne per person.

With continued, if uneven, economic growth the middle-income consumers – the nearly two billion people living in the rapidly expanding economies of Asia (particularly China and India), South and Central America (especially Brazil and Mexico), eastern Europe and a small part of Africa – will be of great importance to future carbon dioxide emissions. If they achieve the consumption patterns of today's rich, there would be no hope of stabilising, let alone reducing, global carbon dioxide emissions. The only way of stabilising carbon dioxide emissions, and allowing the poorest to raise their standard of living to the middle-income level, would be for the future rich to reduce their carbon dioxide emissions by at least 60 per cent. For such global equity, energy consumption by the rich would have to be

(a)

(b)

(c)

Figure 26   (a) The rich. (b) The middle-income consumer, aspiring to a better lifestyle. (c) The poor.
Sources: (a) John Foxx/Alamy; (b) Kevin Foy/Alamy; (c) Greenshoots Communications/Alamy

reduced by perhaps 25 to 35 per cent. As the energy analyst Vaclav Smil so passionately argues:

> Such reductions would call for nothing more than a return to levels that prevailed just a decade or no more than a generation ago [Figure 27]. How could one even use the term sacrifice in this connection? Did we live so unbearably 10 or 30 years ago that the return to those consumption levels cannot be even publicly contemplated by serious policy makers because they feel, I fear correctly, that the public would find such a suggestion unthinkable and utterly unacceptable?

(Smil, 2003, p. 338)

Figure 27   Global equity would require a return to the living standards of the 1970s Source: Topfoto

To achieve such reductions in energy and carbon dioxide emissions would require not only changes in technology towards non-fossil fuels, but also radical changes in consumption patterns towards a low-energy lifestyle. Is it possible to achieve such fundamental shifts in consumer behaviour? To answer such a question requires an understanding of the social and psychological roots of consumption.

SAQ 7

(a) By what factor do the average carbon dioxide emissions of the rich exceed those of the poor?

(b) Why are the middle-income peoples so crucial to future projections of global carbon dioxide emissions?

4.2 Social aspects of consumption

The *Markets* block introduced you to people's attitudes to consumption and advertisers' attempts to influence consumer behaviour. This section takes the discussion further by attempting to summarise the large and diverse literature on the role of consumption in people's lives, and the difficulties encountered by appeals to consume less. As people get wealthier their social and psychological needs for status, love and respect become more important than their basic material needs for food, shelter and clothing. They then seek consumption that can actually help achieve these non-material and social objectives, and purchase goods and services that convey status and social position. It is at this point that ideas of good taste and bad taste become important, rationalised as better designed, higher quality or even organic. These ideas are used to establish a person's social position and to show they are or are not a member of a particular group.

Much as many people would like to change their lifestyle towards a simpler and less stressful one, this cannot be done easily. Many people are locked into current consumption trends by a combination of past choices (for example marriage and family), technology (for example car commuting), economic incentives (the monthly pay cheque), institutions (a career), psychological traits (for example ambition for promotion) and the cultural and social systems to which they belong (their neighbourhood). Family and friendship groups also constrain choices as they provide rules, norms and assumptions about lifestyles, such as where to live, where to go on holiday and what car to drive.

Yet consumption patterns and lifestyles are continually changing in response to technological and social changes. The car replaced the horse and carriage, and domestic appliances replaced domestic servants (Figure 28). New technologies open up new lifestyle possibilities as computers and mobile phones did when they became widely used. When people understand the negative effects of their behaviour and have sufficient motivation, they can give up harmful habits such as smoking and excessive drinking. And at times of national emergency, whole populations are willing to embrace austerity and accept rationing (Figure 29).

It is most important to remember that consumption has social roots – it is not just about the accumulation of physical objects but also about expressing individuals' lifestyles, values and personal identities. As Jackson and Michaelis remark:

> We consume not just to nourish or protect ourselves or to sustain a living. We consume in order to identify ourselves with a social group, to position ourselves within that group, to distinguish ourselves with respect to other social groups, to communicate allegiance to certain ideals. To differentiate ourselves from certain other ideals. We consume in order to communicate. Through

VALENTINE'S IMPROVED DUST-PAN.

Just guide the Hoover lightly with one hand. No need to bear down on it. It does all the work itself.

(a)   (b)

Figure 28   Changes in domestic and social life: (a) Victorian servant sweeping; (b) 1930s housewife with new electric vacuum cleaner
Source: Mary Evans Picture Library

Figure 29   Wartime ration queue outside confectioner
Source: Popperfoto/Alamy

consumption we communicate not only with each other but with our past, with our ideals, with our fears and with our aspirations. We consume in pursuit of meaning.

(Jackson and Michaelis, 2003, p. 39)

The drive for self-expression in industrialised society is reinforced by the advertising industry, whose ads feature what are considered desirable lifestyles, available through the purchase of commodities, and by signals of approval and disapproval from family, friends and colleagues (Figure 30).

(a)   (b)   (c)

Figure 30   Ads promoting products that promise: (a) desirable lifestyle; (b) approval of friends or family; (c) prestige or self-esteem Sources: (a) BMW AG; (b) Purestock/Alamy; (c) Henry Westheim Photography/Alamy

4.2.1 Creating identity

Consumption can be a way to establish and affirm an individual's identity or self-concept. According to social psychologists the primary motivations for such consumption are people's desire to:

- be viewed in a positive light by themselves and others (self-esteem)

- feel they have control over their lives and their immediate environment (self-efficacy)

- strive for a feeling they are being true to themselves (to feel authentic).

These values are often no longer obtained through work, which is sometimes described as soul-destroying, and instead are sought through consumption. Advertising and marketing therefore persuade consumers to see their identities as linked to a particular brand or product. Brands promote the symbolic power of a product to confer prestige or increase self-esteem, and aim to provide a sense of community and satisfaction.

However, wealth and possessions cannot meet all the needs of the self, and under conditions of extreme emotional stress consumption may be questioned as it no longer provides a source of satisfaction and fulfilment. This identity crisis often arises from traumatic personal or family circumstances, such as redundancy, retirement, divorce, death, or children leaving home. People may then voluntarily decide to consume less in an attempt to gain a new identity. Surveys reveal that one of the main motivations for people deciding to consume less is generally not altruism or environmental concerns, but rather a personal response to a crisis of self-identity (Cohen and Murphy, 2001, p. 186).

As well as playing an important role in constructing and maintaining personal identity, consumerism also occupies a role once fulfilled by religion. It allows people to construct rituals – such as the Sunday visit to the shopping centre or car boot sale – to make sense of their lives, and to protect the ideals they wish to live by. It is relative, rather than absolute, wealth and income that seem to be important to individual well-being. Therefore the level of inequality in a society has a crucial impact on people's satisfaction with their consumption levels – the more equality, the greater the satisfaction with a lower level.

In modern society, then, consumption plays a vital role in articulating social identity, ensuring social capabilities and maintaining social cohesion. People's status and the respect of friends and family come from owning and consuming the right goods. As Jackson and Michaelis comment:

> Here is perhaps the clearest message yet that simplistic appeals to consumers to forgo material consumption will be unsuccessful. Such an appeal is tantamount to demanding that we give up certain key capabilities and freedoms as social beings. Far from being irrational to resist such demands, it would be irrational not to, in such a society.

> (Jackson and Michaelis, 2003, p. 36)

For these reasons governments are extremely wary of issuing appeals for people to cut their consumption and change their behaviour, knowing that such a message will be strongly resisted. The message to consume less will be accepted only if it is portrayed in a positive light, as an expression of desirable virtues. For example, in wartime, rationing can be expressed as a symbol of deeply held values such as patriotism, community solidarity and equality. As Jordan and O'Riordan argue:

> For sustainable consumption to gain hold, sustainability as an ideal will have to be universally valued in society, and in the image of social responsibility. Unless and until consuming sustainably achieves the same moral and social status as consuming unsustainably, any government-led policy to achieve sustainable consumption will be hard pressed to achieve significant results.

> (Jordan and O'Riordan, 2000, p. 93)

4.3 Achieving behavioural change

Sustainable consumption, with its message of consuming less, requires the northern lifestyle be redefined so as to reduce material consumption. This will probably require changes in behaviour and consequently lifestyles. To achieve such changes a range of policies would be needed, from education and moral persuasion to legislation banning certain types of advertisements and perhaps products. The idea of a sustainable lifestyle can appear to many consumers as a restrictive set of practices that ultimately mean having to go without things that make life convenient, particularly those that save time. People's lifestyles are already a valiant attempt to manage often-contradictory influences within one life, such as balancing work with family. While there is a strong reaction against external calls for change there can be a willingness to consider actions that might fit into current patterns.

As discussed above, people's lifestyles are an expression of their identities and beliefs, and so new lifestyles are often rejected because they go against firmly held beliefs about the right or moral way to live. Any departure from existing lifestyles can cause loss of self-esteem and feelings of inadequacy – not being a good enough provider to be able to provide the family with a large-screen television or a big car, for example, or not being green enough and buying non-organic food for children, or having the central heating turned up in a low-energy home. Therefore ethical calls for behavioural change are likely to fail, as they always have.

Only under extreme stress do people change and become willing to alter their lifestyles. Some authoritarian regimes – for example in China during the Cultural Revolution in the 1960s – and some cults use techniques involving extreme psychological pressure to compel people to accept change. However, where there is freedom of choice, compulsion to change is likely to be strongly resisted and seen as an attack on self.

4.3.1 Social dimensions

One successful way to change behaviour is through what is known as the voluntary simplicity movement. This movement consists of small social and community groups where people learn about environmental and social issues, explore lifestyle options and take collective action to reduce consumption. The strength of the movement lies in the mutual support given to group members and their ability to develop their own culture of consumption.

However, there is a limit to the change that can be achieved by these small groups unless there is a change in the wider context of society, markets and infrastructure. Achieving lifestyle change is a political process that requires popular participation together with widespread understanding and interest in environmental issues.

To be successful, the sustainable consumption movement needs to examine, understand and question today's lifestyles. The discussion of sustainable consumption should focus on the non-material social and psychological objectives of consumers: that is, their need for respect, status and autonomy. Advertising and the media are central to this process, and the media could be used to create ideas of glamorous sustainable lifestyles, and to actively encourage people to purchase less environmentally damaging goods and services. It is necessary to remember that every product has intrinsic symbolic properties and the marketing of green products therefore needs to exploit the latest marketing techniques to create strong brands and desirable products (Figure 31).

38

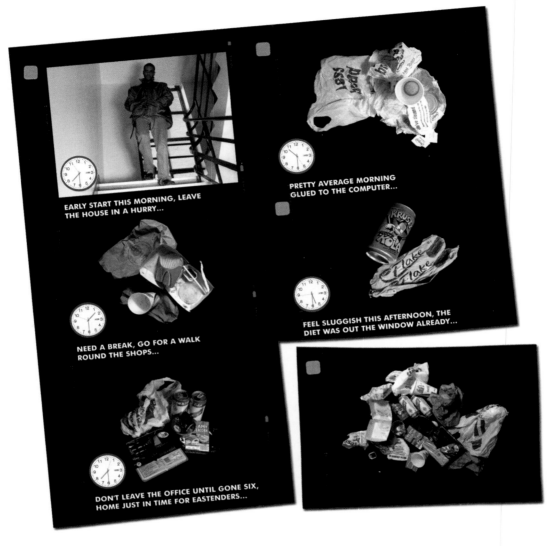

Figure 31   Ad criticising wasteful lifestyle, from the anti-consumption magazine *Ergo* Source: Enzo Peccinotti/ Global Action Plan

SAQ 8

Why do people feel threatened and defensive if they are asked to change their consumption patterns or lifestyle?

The next section looks at a more integrated approach to sustainable products and consumption, which seeks to combine technology and lifestyle issues.

Key points of Section 4

- There are numerous theories of consumer behaviour and social change from a wide range of disciplines.

- It is important to understand the motives of consumers for buying products – this is the foundation of advertising and marketing.

- An understanding of consumer behaviour is an essential feature of any attempts to market green products and lifestyles.

5 Technology and sustainability

This section looks at how people perceive environmental problems, and the possible solutions to such problems: technical, regulatory and behavioural. You will see examples of communities where these combinations of solutions are used to create a more sustainable lifestyle.

5.1 Defining a problem

Innovation for sustainability requires the problems to be identified and then possible solutions to be sought. The perception of the problem is all-important. Whether it is seen as insignificant or life-threatening will determine what solutions are put forward. Unless there is a wide-ranging consensus on the threat posed by a problem there is unlikely to be effective action. People's responses to environmental problems from global climate change to local traffic noise vary from dismissal to enthusiasm. The spectrum of responses to environmental problems may be summed up as follows:

- denial – 'it's media hype'

- indifference – 'it doesn't affect me' or 'it's someone else's problem'

- laissez-faire – 'it will work itself out' or 'it will solve itself'

- technical fix – 'technology will solve the problem'

- government regulation – 'the government will do something'

- behavioural change – 'we should change our behaviour and adopt a sustainable lifestyle'.

The perceived severity of some environmental problems depends on geographical location. For example, traffic congestion may be a problem in London or Edinburgh but not in the Highlands of Scotland. Building a new airport in Essex directly affects those nearby but not those 250 kilometres away.

Denial and indifference (Figure 32a) are common responses to environmental problems. Firstly, people are not convinced by the evidence, scientific or other, which is generally not unanimous. Secondly, people do not see the problem as affecting them personally: they are distanced from it geographically and socially. Thirdly, the distribution of the costs and benefits of some problems, such as climate change, is not uniform: some people may welcome the effects of the problem – for example, warmer drier summers in Britain – and be indifferent to other costs such as storms, water shortage and biodiversity loss.

Even when people recognise there is a problem they may still decide that no action needs to be taken. This generally fatalistic view is based on the belief that there are natural or social forces beyond their control that will correct the problem. Some believe in market forces, others in science; others think solutions will appear and the world can muddle through.

For those who accept there is a problem there are three types of solution: technical, regulatory and behavioural or lifestyle. The enthusiasm with which each element is embraced depends on individual perceptions of the nature of the problem, but ultimately on a collective vision of what society should be like now and in the future (Figure 32b).

(a)   (b)

Figure 32 Contrasting views of the local environment: (a) a lack of concern; (b) a collective action Sources: (a) Janine Wiedel Photolibrary/Alamy; (b) Topfoto

Those people who value personal mobility highly are likely to oppose attempts to restrict car and plane travel, and will therefore seek technical solutions. In contrast, those who value the unspoilt countryside will probably oppose wind turbines or new road and airport construction, and seek restrictions on growth in car and plane travel, possibly through regulatory means. Finally, those opposed to material growth, such as many 'deep greens' or radical environmentalists, will propose lifestyle changes that lead to less need to travel.

One proposed solution is to innovate a way out of this problem, perhaps by developing cars that run on non-fossil fuels, such as hydrogen produced from electricity generated by nuclear reactors or from solar energy. Another technical solution would be to reduce the need for private cars by developing new and better forms of public transport. Yet another would be to lessen the need to travel by using information and communication technology (ICT) to work from home or to create virtual worlds that people could tour from their homes. In contrast to these technological solutions are social and political innovations that seek to limit or manage car use, either through group measures such as car-sharing schemes or through national decisions such as road pricing. Finally there is the regulatory approach, which is explored further below.

The type of solution proposed, and the innovations required to implement it, depends on society's attitudes to consumption. Is growth in consumption associated with growth in quality of life and happiness? Is the end in life more material possessions and the services that go with them? Or are there more important things in life, such as the non-material joys of relationships with family and friends and personal satisfaction achieved through artistic or educational achievements?

5.2   Combined approach

In dealing with most environmental problems a combination of at least two of the three approaches may be required, and the most complex problem of all, climate change, will most probably require all three.

Consider the introduction of a new technology. This frequently requires a new regulatory structure – think about mobile phones, satellite television and genetically modified organisms or GMOs – to set technical standards, allow access to consumer markets and obtain public support. New technologies also have an impact on lifestyles, creating the need for consumers to have sufficient money to purchase and use the technology, the training to know how to use it and the infrastructure to allow them to access it.

An example from the late nineteenth century is cars, which were then a new technology. Initially highway regulations in Britain restricted their speed (Figure 33) and gave preference to horses – the dominant mode of road travel at the time. Not until regulations were amended in their favour did use of cars expand, helped greatly by lifestyle choices that welcomed the freedom of mobility and the privacy the car brought in comparison to public transport.

Figure 33   Early cars had their speed strictly limited by having to follow a walker with a red flag Source: National Motor Museum/MPL

Regulation is often used to force the pace of technology to find solutions to problems and this has particularly been the case with environmental legislation. Regulation also imposes restrictions on lifestyle. People are required to be law-abiding, that is to obey rules and regulations on what and how they consume – no drugs or guns, don't drink and drive, obey the speed limits, no coal fires, don't build that house there. Some regulations, such as building standards and planning controls, can inhibit innovations in low-energy homes and communities. However, overall in modern northern societies that believe in freedom of choice, the law protects people's freedom to consume and so it is not politically easy to prohibit consumption that is considered unsustainable. Politicians cannot ban people from driving their cars or using planes or consuming fossil fuels – all they can do is make these things more difficult through restrictions, or more expensive through taxes, or unattractive by offering better alternatives such as public transport or virtual reality.

Lifestyle choices create a demand for a wide variety of technologies and products from the mainstream to the bizarre – solar panels and windmills for the self-sufficient, iPods for music addicts, mobile phones for those always wanting to be in touch, or flotation tanks and crystals for the spiritually focused. Regulation also helps to protect lifestyle choices by providing legal status and financial assistance to individuals and families, and to voluntary and community groups. For example, in 2006 the DTI's Low Carbon Buildings programme was introduced, offering grants to householders and communities for the installation of micro-generation technologies.

micro-generation

generation of electricity on a small scale, using technologies such as micro-wind turbines and solar panels

SAQ 9

Name a technology whose diffusion has been expedited by regulation and list the types of assistance given by that regulation.

5.2.1 Technology optimist or pessimist?

The preferred approach to environmental problems in market economies over the last 50 years has been the combination of technology and regulation. From the Clean Air Act of 1956 onwards, regulation has generally been required to force the introduction of new technologies against the wishes of vested industrial interests and an indifferent, and sometimes hostile, public.

This approach is well suited to tackling pollution from a few point sources, such as large industrial plants, but is less suitable for dealing with environmental problems caused by millions of consumers wanting to use energy, drive their cars and fly abroad. Another approach, which combines technological and behavioural change, may be necessary. The preferred solution often depends on whether you are a technology optimist or pessimist. Is using technology the answer or the problem?

This fault line has existed for over a century and is much debated by critics of society. It is also reflected in science fiction literature. For example, there is the technological optimism of Arthur C. Clarke in the early 1950s about space travel and of Kim Stanley Robinson in the late 1980s about the colonisation of Mars. This is countered by the pessimism of Harry Harrison in the mid-1960s with his view of a hellish future for humanity in an overcrowded polluted world. There is also the ambiguity of Ursula LeGuin in the mid-1970s, who sees technology being used to create either a flawed ecotopia or an oppressive society. Figure 34 shows representations of some visions of the future.

ecotopia

this term comes from an influential book by Callenbach (1975) and is a compound of 'ecological' and 'utopia'

Similar scenarios are seen in the academic discussion of environmental problems. To the technological optimists – for example, economists and writers such as Herman Kahn, Julian Simon and Bjorn Lomborg – the world is becoming a better place and environmental problems are being solved. While there are still problems such as global warming, these can be overcome by the application of technology and regulation.

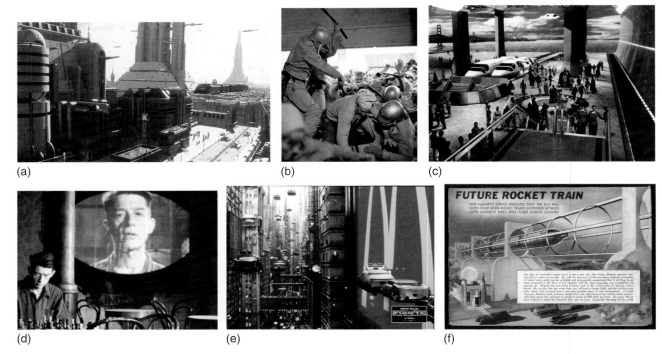

Figure 34   Visions of the future: (a) futuristic architecture in *Star Wars*; (b) hellish dystopia of *Soylent Green*; (c) space travel in *Star Trek*; (d) the totalitarian state of *1984*; (e) an overcrowded city in *The Fifth Element*; (f) rocket-powered train predicted in the 1930s Sources: (a) 20th Century Fox/Lucas Films; (b) Ronald Grant; (c) Paramount Pictures; (d) Umbrella-Rosenblum Films Production; (e) Gaumont; (f) Mary Evans Picture Library; (a)–(e) provided by the Ronald Grant Archive

However to longstanding environmental writers – such as Paul Ehrlich and Barry Commoner, who started writing in the mid 1960s – and more modern environmentalists – such as Ted Trainer and Richard Douthwaite – technology is not the answer as it leads only to more resource consumption and hence more environmental problems. Their solutions are regulation and lifestyle changes.

Overall, environmental writers and activists have gained a reputation as technological pessimists, with early writers being labelled as prophets of doom in the early 1970s. However some environmentalists, such as members of the alternative technology movement, attempted to put forward a more constructive approach and develop new types of technology suited to a more ecological lifestyle based on small, self-sufficient communities.

Proposed solutions for environmental problems reflect these underlying views on the role of technology. Pessimists argue that technology will not solve the problems for the following reasons:

- People in the north live in a society committed to growth and consumerism, so they won't consume less even if they consume greener products and services.

- Developing countries in the south (poor countries) have a right to expand their consumption and will do so. Therefore efforts by countries in the north will be swamped by the economic and population growth of the south.

- More efficient resource use – that is, greater eco-efficiency – just leads to more consumption because of the rebound effect.

- The world has natural environmental limits, so if humanity is to survive it is imperative to respect these.

In contrast, the optimists point out:

- Historically the ingenuity of humans has achieved rapid technical and social change, especially under pressure.

- There has been rapid development of greener, more efficient technologies, which have replaced older, more polluting ones: for example, condensing gas boilers rather than coal, oil and gas heating systems; renewable energy sources rather than fossil fuels; email and the internet rather than letters and catalogues.

- It is possible to dematerialise production and use, for example through nanotechnology (see the *Invention and innovation* block); there is also a move to service economies based on minimising resource flows.

- Rapid social and behavioural change can occur if suitable technical alternatives are created, such as flexible working hours and working at home using ICT.

- Humanity has always overcome natural limits, and perhaps will in time, if necessary, emigrate to other worlds, starting with the Moon and Mars.

SAQ 10

Which two factors have caused the technological pessimists to be proved wrong so far?

5.3   Changing energy sources

To meet its target of a 60 per cent reduction in carbon dioxide emissions by 2050 the UK government is proposing a range of strategies, including greater eco-efficiency and more renewable energy technologies. As I discussed in Section 3 eco-efficiency has its limitations: economic growth always seems to outpace efficiency improvements. The other main strategy – to replace fossil fuels with fossil-free alternatives such as renewable energy sources and/or nuclear power – avoids direct emissions. Of course resources are needed to build the plants and, in the case of nuclear, to fabricate the fuel and deal with the subsequent wastes. Even so, to varying degrees, zero-carbon energy technologies at least partly escape the emission limits on consumption.

As discussed in the *Diffusion* block, the UK government has a target for 20 per cent of its electricity to be generated from renewable energy sources such as wind, wave and solar power by 2020. However, there is opposition to wind power from some regional conservation organisations and local countryside protection groups. Although these plants do not use any polluting energy sources, objectors argue that they have other environmental and social impacts. A particular source of local hostility is resentment about big and remote power companies imposing wind farm projects on local communities. A solution to this is to have small locally owned projects, which can then share directly in the benefits of wind farms as well as the costs. Local ownership in the form of cooperatives is likely to be popular in communities that are already aware of ecological issues and want to find local solutions to energy problems.

This is what has happened widely in Denmark, where around 80 per cent of the wind projects are locally owned by groups such as wind cooperatives, as discussed in the *Diffusion* block. One result is that, unlike the situation in the UK, there has been little local opposition to wind power and some communities are eager to become totally self-sufficient in energy (see Box 4).

Box 4   Renewable energy on Samsø Island

In 1997 the residents of Samsø, a small Danish island off the east coast of the Jutland Peninsula, embarked on an ambitious attempt to eliminate all use of fossil fuels by the end of 2008. Although all 4000 residents were invited to be involved in this project, most of the work was done by the 350 members of an island cooperative, which provided a way for local people to own shares in the project. Samsø, which earns most of its income from tourism and its annual music festival, is hoping this project will attract new industries and bring new jobs. The island cooperative runs most of the wind generators (Figure 35) and supplies heat for households but some of the wind turbines are owned by individuals and one by an investment company.

Figure 35   Wind turbines in operation Source: Skyscan/Science Photo Library

This project involved switching over to the use of wind turbines and having local heating systems powered by solar energy and biomass fuels derived from farm products. It was also hoped to replace petrol vehicles with electric-powered and eventually fuel-cell cars. By 2002 eleven 1 MW wind turbines had been installed, meeting the island's electrical needs. Subsequently four district heating networks were set up, one of them using heat from 2500 m^2 of solar collectors and another with heat from a biogas plant. In 2003 a 23 MW wind farm was installed 7 km off the coast, using 2.3 MW Bonus machines, at a cost of 32.2 million euro.

These facilities allow excess power to be exported to the mainland and so balance any power that has to be imported. It also provides enough power to offset that used by the ferries linking the island to the mainland, and by the vehicles used on the island. So the island is in effect carbon neutral. In the longer term there are plans to introduce electric vehicles on the island and to build a hydrogen-producing wind plant to provide power for some vehicles. The island will then be totally self-sufficient.

The idea of local-level generation does not have to stop with community-based wind, solar or biomass projects. It could involve local combined heat and power (CHP) schemes for conventional homes, as in Woking (see the *Diffusion* block), or for specially designed low-energy housing projects such as at BedZED, Findhorn and Hockerton.

This would be a good time to view the videos 'Community generation: Samsø Island', 'Green housing' (BedZED) and 'Findhorn' and 'Hockerton' in the 'Green lifestyles' section, which are associated with this block on the T307 DVD. You might also find it useful to review the 'Local generation: Woking' video that you watched as part of the *Diffusion* block.

5.3.1 Low-energy housing

Low-energy housing projects are developments that use technology and innovative design to achieve low- or zero-carbon homes and communities. Such projects do this through various combinations of high levels of insulation and high-performance glazing, with heating provided by passive solar gain and incidental gains from people and appliances often backed up by CHP systems, as well as contributions from wind and solar power (Figure 36). In addition there are often shared facilities such as home working, recreation and transport, including car clubs (see below).

The five houses of Hockerton (see Box 5 and the 'Green lifestyles' video) make up one of the first such schemes, but low-energy housing ideas are being incorporated into more mainstream developments such as BedZED and the Ecopark, which are both in the London suburbs. Ecopark is part of the new Thamesmeade urban village of over 1500 new homes, shops and a school arranged around a central ecological corridor. It is an affordable housing scheme of 39 two-, three- and four-bedroom houses, and its developers claim its aim is to 'demonstrate that sustainable living isn't something new and cutting-edge, needing a huge effort and an immense budget' (Gallions Housing Association, undated). The homes contain a combination of cost-effective energy-efficiency measures and sustainable principles:

- timber frame construction

- high level of insulation and advanced double-glazed windows

- condensing boilers and solar water heating

- water-saving features such as low-flush toilets, special spray taps and smaller baths

- energy-efficient lighting

(a)   (b)   (c)

(d)   (e)

Figure 36 **Small-scale renewables: (a) home-built wind generator; (b) solar cells on a house roof; (c) Hockerton Housing Project; (d) BedZED; (e) Gallions Ecopark** Sources: (a) Robin Scagell/Science Photo Library; (b) Martin Bond/Science Photo Library; (c) Hockerton Housing Project; (d) Zedfactory.com; (e) Gallions Housing Association

- waste separation facilities in the kitchens to assist recycling
- under-floor heating and mechanical ventilation with heat recovery.

Box 5   Hockerton ecological housing

The Hockerton Housing Project near Nottingham is the UK's first earth-sheltered, self-sufficient ecological housing development. Its five houses are some of the most energy-efficient purpose-built dwellings in Europe. The residents generate their own energy, harvest their own water and recycle their waste materials, causing minimal pollution and carbon dioxide emissions; their electricity is generated from two wind turbines and photovoltaic cells.

In January 2005 a new eco-community building was completed, with the aim of providing better facilities for visitors and more effectively demonstrating the key sustainability principles of the project. The key features of this 'sustainable resource centre' are:

- floors with 200 mm insulation
- walls (facing bricks fired from waste methane) with 250 mm insulation
- earth-covered roof with 500 mm insulation
- high-specification doors and windows
- floors tiled for longevity and low energy use over the life cycle
- compost toilets and waterless urinals
- environment-friendly paints and varnishes on all surfaces

- recycled furniture and kitchen fittings
- solar thermal system integrated with a novel thermal store.

Exercise 1   Calculate your ecological footprint

On the course website you will find a link to a website where you can calculate your own ecological footprint. Compare the results of your calculation with the footprints of the residents of BedZED.

These housing projects rely on mainly technical solutions to produce homes with low energy use and minimal carbon emissions. The technical solutions they adopt are available to all homeowners in existing buildings and a much greater number of people could be helped to reduce their emissions by installing embedded energy generation systems – photovoltaic solar on the roof top, micro-CHP units in the kitchen and fuel cells in the garage (see the *Diffusion* block).

Moving to fossil-free fuels is a potentially straightforward technical solution to the problem of climate change, and such a move is now under way. However, as I mentioned earlier, even fossil-free fuels have environmental impacts, particularly on land use. Does society want an ever-increasing land area covered with wind farms, biomass plantations or solar cells? There may be local and ultimately global limits to the amount of energy that can be produced from renewable sources because of their environmental impacts, and in the long term it may be necessary to curb the rising demand for energy. So in what other ways can energy use be cut? Is the behavioural approach appropriate?

5.4   Changing behaviour

There are already well-established regulatory approaches to reducing energy consumption, such as energy taxes, building regulations and even rationing in emergencies. However, raising energy prices and curbing consumption are politically unpopular measures. So what about the behavioural approach? Are people willing to reduce their consumption? A poll for the BBC in July 2004 (see Box 6) found that most people – 85 per cent – said they were willing to make some behavioural changes to tackle climate change, but two-thirds were unwilling to pay more for petrol.

Box 6   BBC poll on climate change and consumption

Climate change came last of the list of important issues facing the UK, chosen by 53%, though 64% said it was one of the most important problems facing the world. ... Asked whether changes in personal behaviour would make a difference, 54% said yes and 44% no. Despite that, 85% said they would be prepared to make changes, with only 13% dissenting. The changes people were prepared to make included recycling more household waste (96%), using less energy at home (92%), using cars less (68%), and taking fewer flights (62%). But only 51% said they would be prepared to pay more to fly, and just 37% would agree to pay more for petrol.

Kirby, 2004 [online]

A report from the National Consumer Council (2003), *Green Choice – What Choice?*, looked at consumers' attitudes to sustainable consumption. The NCC found that consumers have a positive but passive view of sustainable consumption. They are generally happy to do their bit towards sustainable consumption – to be responsible – but convenience in their pressured daily lives takes precedence. The report's key findings were as follows.

- Priority – Everyone has more immediate and pressing concerns than sustainable consumption.

- Habit and inconvenience – Consumers see habit as a barrier to change and are honest about their unwillingness to change their habits.

- Cost – Attitudes to cost are complex and often mask other barriers of inconvenience and lack of awareness.

- Awareness – While consumers say they know how to behave sustainably, discussions show they have low awareness of the effect of their daily lives on the environment, and of sustainable consumption policies, facilities and products.

- Lack of access to facilities – Facilities to recycle, save energy, travel and shop sustainably could be improved for all consumers. There are particular difficulties for low-income consumers who have fewer household recycling facilities, rely on landlords for housing repairs and, in some areas, have infrequent, unsafe public transport.

5.4.1 Positive behaviour

Despite the rather negative picture above there is some hope. It has been found that consumers' attitudes to sustainable consumption can be influenced by their adoption of new technologies, such as rooftop photovoltaic solar and micro wind turbines (see the *Diffusion* block). A recent report for the Sustainable Consumption Roundtable (a joint initiative of the National Consumer Council and the Sustainable Development Commission) looked at how the adoption of domestic-scale micro-generation technologies affected behaviour (Dobbyn and Thomas, 2005). It found the visible presence of wind turbines and sun panels around the home provides a tangible reminder of energy use, which also works to change behaviours. It led many to consider other changes, including changes to their lifestyle.

This sort of outcome was, unsurprisingly, more marked for people who actively chose to install the systems, in contrast to people who simply moved into houses where such systems were already installed or where the system was installed for them as part of a local council programme. But even the late, relatively passive, experience 'rarely leaves families unchanged in their outlook and behaviour' (p. 2).

The report compared these outcomes with the situation for mainstream consumers – the majority – who had not had this experience, and concluded that:

> The language of 'energy efficiency in the home' is currently going over the heads of householders who do not make the links between their TVs, dishwashers and thermostats and their active concern about global climate change. Making energy generation part and parcel of people's homes and schools may hold the key to empowering and engaging energy consumers for the first time.
>
> (Dobbyn and Thomas, 2005, p. 3)

Of course, for changes in attitude of this type to become prevalent, widespread adoption by consumers of the new energy technologies would be required. However, it does seem that interest in this area is growing. A survey published by The Co-operative Bank (2005) found that 'consumers are increasingly taking it upon themselves to tackle climate change, spending £3.4 billion in the process. On average, this equates to some £140 per household' (p. 3). This 2004 figure represented a 21 per cent increase on 2003. Sales of energy-efficient appliances went up by 23 per cent, while expenditure on micro-generation increased more than fourfold to £23 million. The survey also found that two-thirds (66 per cent) of consumers covered had considered the environmental impact of their spending when making purchasing decisions, up from 55 per cent in 2003, and 1 in 10 people said they used public transport for environmental reasons.

5.4.2 EcoTeam approach

One organisation that is tackling the kinds of problems identified in the NCC report is the environmental charity Global Action Plan (GAP), which sets out explicitly to encourage a change in lifestyle through awareness raising and dialogue. It adopts a collective, community-based strategy called the EcoTeam approach.

This involves a group of 6 to 10 people who might be neighbours or members of the same religious organisation or members of some interest group or club. They meet once a month and discuss ideas, experiences and achievements related to the EcoTeam programme (Figure 37). The eight-month programme is based on a workbook that addresses six areas in turn: waste, gas, electricity, water, transport and consumption. The workbook explains each theme, the goals of GAP and a number of actions that can be taken by households to reach those goals. The emphasis is on the household rather than the individual, so that EcoTeam members work with other household members to change behaviour.

The most detailed evaluation of the EcoTeam approach has been in the Netherlands, where EcoTeams have typically achieved reductions in car use and consumption of energy and water of around 10 per cent, and reductions in waste of around 40 per cent. Similar results have been achieved in the UK. It was found that participants were most likely to maintain behavioural changes if they were motivated by a strong and positive link to personal meaning and identity. To spread its message GAP used to publish a glossy monthly magazine *Ergo*, which aimed to use the top creative minds in the advertising industry

Figure 37 A GAP EcoTeam shares ideas Source: Janine Wiedel Photolibrary/ Alamy

to promote green and ethical consumption, and to show that such a lifestyle can be fashionable and glamorous.

This would be a good time to view the video 'Global Action Plan: action in schools', which is associated with this block on the T307 DVD.

5.4.3 Personal carbon rationing

The experiences of such groups as Global Action Plan in achieving behavioural changes would be important if the UK government ever introduced radical measures, such as personal carbon rationing (Figure 38), in order to achieve its goal of a 60 per cent cut in carbon dioxide emissions by 2050.

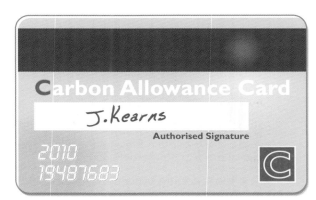

Figure 38 Possible future carbon allowance card Source: adapted from Fawcett, 2004

Personal carbon rations would cover all household energy use and personal transport energy use including air travel – that is, all direct use of energy by individuals – and there would be equal carbon rations for all adults. Those people who invest in household efficiency and renewables, travel less and lead lives with a lower energy input would not need all of their ration and would therefore have a surplus to sell. Those who travel a lot or who live in large or inefficient homes would need to buy this surplus to permit them to continue with something like their accustomed lifestyle. People could therefore trade carbon, and trading would become an integral part of a carbon-rationing scheme.

The carbon rations would gradually decrease over time, both in response to the need to reduce global emissions and to allow for the expected rise in national population. This would have severe consequences for international travel because, for example, just one return flight from London to Athens could exceed the whole personal carbon ration for the year in 2030 (Hillman and Fawcett, 2004).

For such a policy to work consumers would have to be given extensive information about the carbon content of all goods and services they purchase and about the existence of alternatives to carbon-intensive activities such as flying. Carbon rationing might be thought unrealistic in this age of consumer choice and freedom, but it may become a necessary emergency measure in the future when there is rapid climate change requiring drastic and rapid cuts in global carbon emissions.

5.4.4 Car clubs

Another, less radical way to bring a change in lifestyles, discussed in the *Products* block, is through the sharing of goods and services. In a car club (Figure 39) a fleet of cars is available to individuals, who pay according to the distance driven. The idea is that there are environmental benefits when cars are shared. In comparison with privately owned cars, club cars are serviced more regularly by the operator, which increases their efficiency; the cars are updated as increasingly efficient models become available, which is possible because they are used more intensively; and individual customers tend to drive less, using public transport or bicycles for short trips.

Figure 39   Road sign demonstrating the preferential parking system for a car-share scheme Source: CityCarClub

About 125 000 people use car clubs in Europe, and another 60 000 in North America. In Europe they are most widespread in Switzerland, the Netherlands and parts of Germany, but at the time of writing are just starting in the UK. Mobility, a nationwide organisation in

Switzerland, has over 50 000 members operating in 400 towns, compared with fewer than 1000 members belonging to CityCarClub (formerly Smart Moves), the biggest of about 25 car clubs in the UK. CityCarClub was established in 2000 and now has a fleet of over 70 cars in towns and cities across the UK, including Edinburgh, Bristol, London and Brighton.

Another car club in the UK is WhizzGo in Leeds, which operates under a 10-year contract with the city council and aims to be part of the city-wide transport network. There is a £25 joining fee, an hourly rate of between £4 and £5 under a choice of price plans, 10 miles free for each hour, and 20p per mile thereafter including petrol. Members can pre-book by phone or internet to pick up a Citroen C3 at its specified reserved parking bay, and swipe a smart card to trigger the onboard computer to unlock it. Members qualify for discounts on local transport season tickets, and the aim is to tie in their car club usage with more public transport journeys, while halving their travel costs compared with owning a car. In London a similar scheme from the Streetcar club offers its customers cars from 35 pick-up points for £4.95 an hour, including fuel for up to 30 miles; after that the cost is 19p per mile.

5.4.5 Downshifting

Living in a low-energy house or car sharing is no guarantee of living a low-energy lifestyle: the savings on heating or transport bills might be spent on flying abroad for exotic holidays. It is the total expenditure or consumption – largely determined by income – that dictates someone's environmental impact or ecological footprint. Poor people and countries have less of a footprint than rich people and countries. One solution, advocated by deep greens such as Ted Trainer and Richard Douthwaite, is downshifting or adopting what is termed voluntary simplicity – that is, voluntarily reducing consumption of materials and energy through a lifestyle approach based on earning and consuming less. This might involve living in small self-sufficient communities that use renewable energy, grow their own food, and produce and trade their own goods and services. The idea is to have a better quality of life rather than higher material consumption.

Downshifting, often involving an escape to the countryside (Figure 40), rests on the theory that quality of life is becoming increasingly divorced from economic growth, which does not take account of the cost of crime, pollution and environmental degradation. It finds expression in alternative indicators of economic welfare such as the measure of domestic progress used by the New Economics Foundation. By this calculation quality of life was highest in the mid-1970s (Jackson, 2004). Downshifting is not motivated solely by environmental concerns. Generally it is motivated by the desire to trade highly paid jobs involving long hours of work and commuting for less stressful and shorter working hours, and to spend more time on family life.

Downshifting need not be long-term or permanent – it can be seen as a short-term career break involving part-time working because of family commitments rather than ecological concerns. Some people will return to their highly paid careers later when they no longer want or need to trade lower income for more leisure.

Figure 40   Typical derelict French property that appeals to English downshifters Source: Prestige Property Group

So can society consume less by working less and having more leisure time? Historically people in the north have chosen more income rather than more leisure, and downshifting is likely to remain, as it always was, a minority activity. Countryside living can be one vision for a green future but overall the emphasis, if sustainability is to be achieved, will have to be on cities where the majority of people live. Visions for these will have to concentrate on new ways of living, working and travelling, as seen in the SusHouse project (Figure 41), and these are the themes for science fiction and imaginative stories. See Appendix A, 'A Day in the Life', for one vision of a future lifestyle.

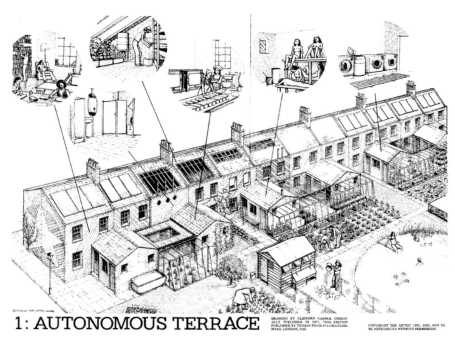

1: AUTONOMOUS TERRACE

Figure 41   1970s vision of new ways to live in urban areas Source: Clifford Harper

5.5   Achieving sustainable innovation

In this block you have been confronted by some moral and ethical questions about the way people in industrialised societies consume.

There is at present a growing awareness of the unsustainability of current patterns of consumption and the need to find ways of tackling the thorny issues of environmental impacts, economic and population growth, and technological change. The lack of greater action or commitment on the part of governments to tackle such problems is sometimes referred to as the *implementation gap*. The reluctance of those in power to embrace change is partly a result of their fear they will lose power by upsetting voters with unpopular measures. There are only so many policy levers and so many combinations of fiscal and regulatory levers that governments can pull.

The magic ingredient in technology innovation and diffusion is creativity. This is frequently expressed in design – perhaps the most powerful tool or human response available to square the circle. All too often products, processes and systems have been designed or have evolved with no or little attention given to sustainability. This is called the *attention deficit*. There is every possibility that good design will redress the attention deficit of many processes and thereby contribute towards bridging the political implementation gap.

What can designers and technologists do to help achieve a sustainable world? The answer is, probably a great deal. Design and innovation could play a central role in delivering sustainable solutions, as environmental impacts are a consequence of what things are made from, and how they are constructed, used and disposed of.

The challenge is to develop radical concepts of sustainable design and sustainable innovation in which the function of the product is considered and alternative, environmentally sustainable means for providing it are examined. Sustainable design approaches range from innovations in technology and new patterns of ownership such as leasing that enable products to be returned to their manufacturer for refurbishing, to radical changes such as shared or communal use of products, replacing the product with a dematerialised service, or even questioning whether the product or function is really needed. Sustainable design and innovation involves moving from the ecodesign of individual products to the ecological design of whole *systems*. Pick up your pencils and computer mice – they are weapons of mass construction and your country needs you now.

As you saw on the T307 DVD and in the *Products* block, the ecodesigner Edwin Datschefski believes that a focus on the materials used could be the answer for sustainable design and it is necessary to start thinking about the 100 per cent sustainable product, 'using materials that are not just less bad but totally good' (Figure 42). He believes that industrial systems need to adopt the protocols of material flow used by nature and, where desirable, to integrate natural and manufactured ecosystems – see Box 7. This approach of assessing materials over their total life cycle is used by The Natural Step, an organisation that helps businesses move in a sustainable direction.

Figure 42   Backpack with solar cells attached, designed by Edwin Datschefski Source: Voltaic Systems/Natural Collection

---

Box 7   Protocols of nature

I summarise the protocols of nature in three words – cyclic, solar and safe. That's cyclic as in materials continually reused, solar as in powered by the sun, and safe as in nothing goes where it shouldn't. Industry has already been adopting these protocols to some extent, and most environmental legislation is derived from them.

As for integrating natural and manmade [sic] ecosystems, industry does already form an ecosystem of sorts – a set of interacting flows of materials and energy. It's not yet a particularly good one, though, as it's not self-sustaining, with open input and output loops. With better integration, the outputs from industry should become the food for natural systems. At the moment they are poison rather than food. But with care and vision, the global industrial system can be redesigned to be 100% cyclic, solar and safe.

(Datschefski, 2004, p. 44)

This block has asked what is wrong with the way people in the north consume. It has argued that present patterns of consumption are unsustainable – Earth is a finite planet and cannot support six billion people at current northern levels of consumption. So what can be done? The *Products* block showed it is possible to develop more efficient ways of using resources, to lower the impacts of using them, and to produce cleaner, greener products. But will that be enough? Probably not. It may be necessary to do more than just make a few improvements to the technologies – it may be necessary to adopt new patterns of consumption. This may involve changes in behaviour and lifestyle. So social as well as technological innovation may be needed.

New sustainable technologies can be developed not only by large corporations but also by small-scale, grass-roots activism and consumer initiatives. Indeed, if the technologies are to be really sustainable, appropriate and accepted, consumers and the grass roots have to play a major role. As you saw in the *Diffusion* block, grass-roots initiatives for sustainable development take the form of innovative networks of activists and organisations that develop bottom-up solutions that respond to the local situation and the interests and values of the communities involved. In contrast to conventional, incremental green reforms, grass-roots initiatives seek to practise deeper, alternative forms of sustainable development. The initiatives involve committed activists who often experiment with social innovations as well as using greener technologies and techniques in areas such as housing, renewable energy, food and alternative money. They frequently seek to create new social institutions and systems of provision based upon different values from those of the mainstream. Examples include community renewable-energy initiatives (as at Samsø) and ecological housing (as at Hockerton).

Above all it must be remembered that achieving sustainable consumption is complex and difficult, requiring a multidisciplinary approach. There is a need to combine technical innovation and social design to produce both green technologies and green organisations and lifestyles. To do this, it is necessary to stimulate imaginations to consider possible future worlds where products and services are 100 per cent cyclic, solar and safe.

Key points of Section 5

- Tackling environmental problems requires a combination of technical, regulatory and behavioural or lifestyle solutions.

- Case studies of communities that use a combination of technology and behavioural change show how a more sustainable lifestyle can be achieved.

- Sustainable consumption will probably be achieved only through grassroots initiatives that pioneer bottom-up solutions for sustainable development and have an imaginative vision of what future lifestyles could involve.

Appendix A

A day in the life

The following article by Roger Levett was published in *Town and Country Planning* in 2000. It contains his vision of a future lifestyle.

1 January 2050: Chuffed to be waking up at all today – already 41 at the millennium, I hadn't expected to see the next round-number anniversary of the historically incorrect birthday of a god I don't even believe in! Just shows what the tranquillity, fresh air, good food and daily cycling that you can get in the middle of a big city can do for one's health.

In some ways, life has changed little. I'm still living in the same 1840 brick terraced house in inner London which I bought in 1993. It, and hundreds of thousands like it, have adapted to the changing demands of the last 50 years as easily and comfortably as the previous 160 years, and seen off much of the more recent housing. This area has even accommodated the pipes for neighbourhood heating from the micro-incinerator on the old oilcar garage site to the north and the organic digester plant to the south (called Old Mcdonald's after the traditional Drive-Thru junk food place it replaced). The sash windows were all unobtrusively draughtproofed and secondary glazed by Power to the People Ltd (the energy utility the Angel Neighbourhood Council and six others own) as part of the deal when they put the heat system in. Overall we use a fifth of the fossil fuel we did in 2000.

We responded to PPG379 on incremental urban densification by adding a new top floor. English Heritage had forbidden this for years, but its successor the Built Quality Enhancement Agency stopped pickling old buildings in whatever inconvenient state they had happened to get into, and instead supported changes that enhanced quality. This was a demanding requirement where quality was already high, but when six of us clubbed together to commission a bold new design they were enthusiastically supportive. They provided facilitators to work with all the residents to establish a consensus, gave grants for demolishing three previous low quality top floor extensions, and even took out an Aesthetic Quality Improvement Order to make the one resistant owner comply with what the rest of us had agreed. Result: our Georgian terrace is capped by a stunningly elegant modern glazed pavilion that draws the streetscape together, provides a versatile mix of extra living space, citrus fruit growing and solar water preheating, superinsulates the rooms below, and even collects and filters the rainwater to provide most of our flushing and washing needs.

Losing access to this is the only thing I really regret about letting the top half of the house to the young family next door. But two floors are now plenty for just the two of us. And there were big incentives: the Neighbourhood Council paid all the costs for soundproofing the party floor and opening access through the walls. Living within our Standard Space Entitlement means we don't pay any Excess Space Tax (and therefore get our Council services almost free, cross-subsidised by people who do insist on keeping prime living space underoccupied). And we get priority for booking Neighbourhood Amenities – there's a really stylish flat in the Common House three doors along that we can usually have when friends want to stay, and we had a glorious reception suite in the converted Victorian factory overlooking the canal for the family Christmas lunch. And we still *own* the whole house, and can have the rest of it back at a year's notice if we want.

At 91 one does get absent-minded. The Carbon Warden had to knock us up at 3 this morning – cycling past on his rounds he'd noticed I'd left the sitting room light on. He knew it must be a mistake because I stopped working all night to meet deadlines when I re-retired at 84 (having been tempted back to work at 73 by the Senior Returners tax breaks).

As I sit down to breakfast (yoghurt from the Finsbury Park Friesians, grapes from our own vine, honey from next door's hive and bread delivered by pedivan from Raabs still warm) the Loudspeaker makes the throat-clearing noises that signal it has something to say. We've got ours permanently set to Reticent: it only initiates conversations when there's something really important. (I can't stand the Gregarious setting some people seem to like, with the wretched thing wittering away about anything and nothing all day long. But I suppose lonely people need it now dogs are banned from urban areas.)

But I'm glad it's piped up now. 'You're going to TCPA Policy Council this afternoon, but another storm as bad as the one last November is due between one and four. Do you want to look at Routemaster?' Policy Council is always a nice chance to natter to other old-timers, so I don't want to miss it. But weather is violent these days, I wouldn't even want to walk up to the Tube station in another storm like that one. So I say 'thank you, yes please', and the Routemaster display flashes up on the wall screen. It shows there's a float going right to the ICA, currently passing on the road parallel to mine, and it's got a very fast routing once the driver hands it over to the automatic guide track at the Angel – only eight minutes, I couldn't have cycled it that fast in my prime! Of course they go much faster once they switch from battery to mains power, and presumably it'll tag on to a big train for some of the way, and therefore take priority at the crossroads.

It'll cost me the standard two Favours for any off-peak surface journey into the centre, plus six Favours to whoever originally ordered the float (and will have paid much more to be certain of door to door routing at the time they choose) to divert it to pick me up from my door, plus three Favours to our street's collective account for bringing such a large and disruptive vehicle (they seat up to 18) along what is now a tranquil gravelled lane between extended gardens, only freely open to foot and pedal traffic. I hesitate: the tube would only cost one Favour. But then I remember I've never fully used my rolling annual entitlement to Favours since it increased when I turned 90. So I press 'firm accept', the Routemaster table updates with the revised exact timings, and I ask the Speaker to monitor that Net channel and warn me if they change again if anyone else books on to the float.

While I'm thinking about travel, I suppose I'd better check the trains to visit my grandson. He's going through a rough patch. The competition is now so fierce for really top-flight jobs that even though his teaching practice went well he didn't get tenure as a primary teacher. And with only a Masters degree he couldn't fall back on secondary teaching, which isn't quite so cutthroat. What should I suggest? No point hoping to be a planner or environmental capital enhancer, they're as prestigious and oversubscribed as teaching. But maybe local services management or ecobalancing. Or if all else fails maybe performance auditing – okay, it's a bit of a joke discipline, everyone knows the things that really matter are the ones you can't measure, but at least it's in the public service.

Meanwhile he's had to take some wretched financial services job as a stopgap – derivatives trading, he said, whatever that means. Of course he couldn't afford to stay in Brixton on what that sort of thing pays. He had to give up that lovely flat just off the Railton Road and move out to slumburbia. Bromley! I suppress a shudder. The moment you get off the train there the chemical reek of oilcars hits you, and once you've got past all the tatty banners with their slogans about freedom the whole front of the station is clogged with oilcars for rent, each with a sallow, sullen man with a beer gut waiting hours for a fare. You have to use them – 'freedom' in Bromley means not having any decent transport, that's why housing is so cheap there.

The drivers relieve their frustration by driving with a nauseous swerving and lurching, but concentrating on not throwing up at least distracts you from being too depressed by the slumburbian townscape – the endless rows of separate houses, each with an old oilcar or two under a special awning out in front (people can't afford to drive them but keep them for display), each with barbed wire round the garden to stop the 'neighbours' stealing the vegetables, the motley shacks and sheds people run their businesses out of, the forlorn placards advertising vegetables or oilcar parts or mending things interspersed with the council's posters about enterprise and freedom.

How will I cheer him up? Perhaps I should tell him there was a time – within my own living memory, indeed – when everybody thought that making money out of buying and selling money was actually more valuable than public service? When cities competed to attract companies like the one he works for, and politicians said we were better off if there were more of them? When everywhere was clogged up with oilcars, even my lovely tranquil street in Islington? Or perhaps not. He'd probably just think I was going soft in the head.

(Levett, 2000)

Answers to self-assessment questions

SAQ 1

Why is the role that consumption plays in causing environmental damage such a contentious issue in international debates?

- At the first Earth Summit in 1992 developed countries – the north – would not accept that their consumption was to blame for global environmental problems and did not want this issue discussed.

- Since then discussion on consumption issues has revolved around the concept of sustainable consumption but there is little international agreement on what this means beyond consuming greener or more sustainable products and generally using resources more efficiently.

SAQ 2

List three problems preventing the widespread use of Interface's carpet-leasing scheme.

- Cost of the products – they may have been more expensive than existing conventional products.

- Lack of a market demand – consumers may not have seen or understood the benefits.

- Complexity of lease arrangements.

- Slow take-up of product – carpets need replacing only every decade.

SAQ 3

Reread Section 2 and list five factors that have influenced designers to produce more environmentally friendly products and services. (Other factors that have influenced designers are listed in the *Products* block.)

- The desire, often altruistic, to satisfy consumers' unmet needs.

- To comply with environmental regulations on waste disposal and pollution.

- To achieve competitive advantage, by designing popular new products and services.

- To reduce manufacturing costs and environmental impacts by being more efficient in the use of energy and materials.

- To gain access to, and recognition in, the green or ethical consumer market through marketing green products.

SAQ 4

Name the three components of the rebound effect discussed above, and identify which is most important in the short run and in the long run.

The three components of the rebound effect are:

- the direct rebound or price effect

- the secondary or income effect

- transformational or indirect effects.

The most important effect in the short run is the price effect; in the long run, transformational effects are most important.

SAQ 5

Name three areas where Factor 10 improvements have been achieved.

Factor 10 improvements have been achieved in pig iron and nitrogen fixation, in decarbonisation of energy sources, and in light bulbs and electricity generation.

SAQ 6

What three criticisms have been made of the UK government's approach to sustainability?

- It concentrates only on technological measures such as improving eco-efficiency.

- It ignores questions of the scale and nature of consumption.

- It lacks the political will to curb consumption through lifestyle changes.

SAQ 7

(a) By what factor do the average carbon dioxide emissions of the rich exceed those of the poor?

(b) Why are the middle-income peoples so crucial to future projections of global carbon dioxide emissions?

(a) A factor of 10.

(b) If middle-income peoples achieved the consumption patterns of today's rich there would be no hope of stabilising, let alone reducing, global carbon dioxide emissions.

SAQ 8

Why do people feel threatened and defensive if they are asked to change their consumption patterns or lifestyle?

People's lifestyles or consumption patterns are an expression of their identities and beliefs, so a change to their lifestyle is often rejected because it is contrary to firmly held beliefs about the right or moral way to live.

SAQ 9

Name a technology whose diffusion has been expedited by regulation and list the types of assistance given by that regulation.

My example is mobile phones. The UK government gave a monopoly to providers after an auction of the wavelengths and it regulates the operation of mobile phones through agencies such as Ofcom. There are also bodies that set international technical standards.

SAQ 10

Which two factors have caused the technological pessimists to be proved wrong so far?

- The development of new technologies to counteract existing and potential problems, as with many air and water pollution problems.

- The possibility of rapid social change if a problem is agreed to be an urgent threat, as in wartime or under emergency conditions.

References, further reading and internet resources

Allenby, B. (2003) 'Industrial ecology' in Molella, M. and Bedi, J. (eds), *Inventing for the Environment*, Cambridge, MA, MIT Press.

Brezet, H. and van Hemel, C. (1997) *Ecodesign: A Promising Approach to Sustainable Production and Consumption*, Paris, United Nations Environment Programme.

Callenbach, E. (1975) *Ecotopia: The Notebooks and Reports of William Weston*, Berkeley, CA, Banyan Tree Books.

Cogoy, M. (1999) 'The consumer as a social and environmental actor', *Ecological Economics*, vol. 28, no. 3, pp. 385–398.

Cohen, M. and Murphy, J. (eds) (2001) *Exploring Sustainable Consumption: Environmental Policy and the Social Sciences*, Oxford, Pergamon.

Co-operative Bank (The) (2005) *The Ethical Consumerism Report 2005*, Manchester, The Co-operative Bank. Available from: www.neweconomics.org/gen/z_sys_PublicationDetail.aspx?PID=217 (accessed 1 August 2005).

Datschefski, E. (2004) 'Material whirl', *Green Futures*, no. 48.

de Beer (1998) *Potential for Industrial Energy Efficiency Improvement in the Long Term*, University of Utrecht.

Department for Environment, Food and Rural Affairs (Defra) (2003) *Changing Patterns: UK Government Framework for Sustainable Consumption and Production*, London, Defra. Available from: www.defra.gov.uk/environment/business/scp/ (accessed 1 August 2005).

Department for Transport (2003) *The Future of Air Transport*, London, Department for Transport. Available from: www.dft.gov.uk/stellent/groups/dft_aviation/documents/divisionhomepage/029650.hcsp (accessed 1 August 2005).

Department for Transport (2004a) *Aviation and Global Warming*, London, Department for Transport. Available from: www.dft.gov.uk/stellent/groups/dft_aviation/documents/page/dft_aviation_031850.pdf (accessed 1 August 2005).

Department for Transport (2004b) *Making Car Sharing and Car Clubs Work: A Good Practice Guide*, London, Department for Transport. Available from: www.dft.gov.uk/stellent/groups/dft_susttravel/documents/page/dft_susttravel_035116.pdf (accessed 1 August 2005).

Department of Trade and Industry (DTI) (2005) *UK Energy Sector Indicators*, London, DTI.

Dobbyn, J. and Thomas, G. (2005) *Seeing the light: the Impact of Micro-generation on the Way We Use Energy*, report for the Sustainable Consumption Roundtable. Available from: www.sd-commission.org.uk/publications.php?id=239 (accessed 1 August 2005).

Douthwaite, R. (1996) *Short Circuit: Strengthening Local Economies for Security in an Unstable World*, Totnes, Green Books.

Dunster, B. (2003) *From A to ZED: Realising Zero (Fossil) Energy Developments*, Wallington, Bill Dunster architects ZEDfactory Ltd.

Ehrlich, P. (1968) *The Population Bomb*, New York, Ballantine Books.

Fawcett, T. (2004) 'Carbon rationing and personal energy use', *Energy and Environment*, vol. 15, no. 6, pp. 1067–1083.

Fuad-Luke, A. (2002) *The Eco-Design Handbook*, London, Thames & Hudson.

Gallions Housing Association (undated) (online), www.gallionsecopark.co.uk (accessed 1/8/2005).

Ghazi, P. and Jones, J. (2004) *Downshifting: The Bestselling Guide to Happier, Simpler Living*, London, Hodder & Stoughton.

Global Action Plan (2004) *Consuming Passion: Do We Have to Shop Until We Drop?* London, Global Action Plan.

Hawken, P., Lovins, A. B. and Lovins, L. H. (1999) *Natural Capitalism: The Next Industrial Revolution*, London, Earthscan.

Heap, B. and Kent, J. (eds) (2000) *Towards Sustainable Consumption: A European Perspective*, London, The Royal Society.

Herring, H. (2005) 'Energy efficiency – a critical view', *Energy: the International Journal*, vol. 31, no. 1, pp. 10–20.

Hertwich, E. (2005) 'Consumption and industrial ecology', *Journal of Industrial Ecology*, vol. 9, no. 1–2, pp. 1–6.

Hillman, M. and Fawcett, T. (2004) *How We Can Save the Planet*, London, Penguin.

Jackson, T. (2004) *Chasing Progress: Beyond Measuring Economic Growth*, London, New Economics Foundation. Available from: www.neweconomics.org/gen/z_sys_PublicationDetail.aspx?PID=176 (accessed 1 August 2005).

Jackson, T. and Michaelis, L. (2003) *Policies for Sustainable Consumption*, report to the Sustainable Development Commission. Available from: www.sd-commission.org.uk/publications.php?id=138 (accessed 1 August 2005).

Jordan, A. and O'Riordan, T. (2000) 'The Social Implications of Consumption' in Heap, B. and Kent, J. (eds) *Towards Sustainable Consumption: A European Perspective*, London, The Royal Society.

Kirby, A. (2004) 'Britons unsure of climate costs', *BBC News*, 29 July (online). Available from: news.bbc.co.uk/1/hi/sci/tech/3934363.stm (accessed 1 August 2005).

Kuehr, R. and Williams, E. (eds) (2004) *Computers and the Environment: Understanding and Managing their Impacts*, Dordrecht, Kluwer.

Levett, R. (2000) 'A day in the life', *Town and Country Planning*, vol. 69, no. 1.

Levett, R., Christie, I., Jacobs, M. and Therivel, R. (2003) *A Better Choice of Choice: Quality of life, Consumption and Economic Growth*, London, Fabian Society.

Malthus, T.R. (1970, first published in 1798) *An essay on the principle of population; and, a summary view of the principle of population*, Harmondsworth, Penguin; also available online at www.ac.wwu.edu/~stephan/malthus/malthus.0.html (accessed 9/6/06).

National Consumer Council (2003) *Green Choice: What Choice?*, London, National Consumer Council.

Organisation for Economic Co-operation and Development (OECD) (1997) *Sustainable Consumption and Production: Clarifying the Concepts*, Paris, OECD.

Oldham, J., James, P. and Shaw, B. (2003) *Delivering Resource Productivity: The Service Solution*, London, Green Alliance.

Oslo Roundtable on Sustainable Production and Consumption (1995) *Elements for an International Work Programme on Sustainable Production and Consumption* (online), subsection 1.2. Available from: www.iisd.ca/consume/oslo000.html (accessed 1 August 2005).

Performance and Innovation Unit (2001) *Resource Productivity: Making More with Less*, London, Performance and Innovation Unit, Cabinet Office.

Porritt, J. (2005) *Capitalism: As if the World Matters*, London, Earthscan.

Potter, S. and Parkhurst, G. (2005) 'Transport policy and transport tax reform', *Public Money and Management*, vol. 25, no. 3, pp. 171–178.

Rejeski, D. (2002) 'E-Commerce, the Internet, and the Environment', *Journal of Industrial Ecology*, vol. 6, no. 2, pp. 1–3.

Schor, J. (1992) *The Overworked American: The Unexpected Decline of Leisure*, New York, Basic Books.

Shi, D. (1985). *The Simple Life: Plain Living and High Thinking in American Culture*, New York, Oxford University Press.

Smil, V. (2003) *Energy at the Crossroads: Global Perspectives and Uncertainties*, Cambridge, MA, MIT Press.

Sustainable Development Commission (2004a) 'News Release 033', London, Sustainable Development Commission, 13 April.

Sustainable Development Commission (2004b) *Shows Promise. But Must Try Harder*, London, Sustainable Development Commission. Available from: www.sd-commission.org.uk/publications.php?id=72 (accessed 1 August 2005).

Trainer, T. (1985) *Abandon Affluence*, London, Zed Books.

United Nations (2004) *World Urbanization Prospects: The 2003 Revision*, New York, United Nations.

United Nations Conference on Environment and Development (1992) *Report of the United Nations Conference on Environment and Development*, New York, United Nations.

United Nations Environment Programme (1999) 'Changing consumption patterns', *Industry and Environment*, vol. 22, no. 4 (special issue).

Van den Bergh, J.C.J.M. and Ferrer-i-Carbonell, A. (2000) 'Economic theories of sustainable consumption' in Heap, B. and Kent, J. (eds) *Towards Sustainable Consumption: A European Perspective*, London, The Royal Society.

Venetoulis, J., Chazan, D. and Gaudet, C. (2004) *Ecological Footprint of Nations 2004*, Oakland CA, Redefining Progress. Available from: www.redefiningprogress.org/publications/footprintnations2004.pdf (accessed 1 August 2005).

von Weizsäcker, E. U., Lovins, A. B. and Lovins, L. H. (1997) *Factor Four: Doubling Wealth – Halving Resource Use*, London, Earthscan.

World Commission on Environment and Development (WCED) (1987) *Our Common Future* (Brundtland report), Oxford, Oxford University Press.

Worldwatch Institute (2004) *State of the World 2004*, New York, W.W. Norton.

World Wide Fund for Nature (2004) *Living Planet Report 2004*, Gland, Switzerland, World Wide Fund for Nature. Available from: www.panda.org/news_facts/publications/key_publications/living_planet_report/index.cfm (accessed 1 August 2005).

Internet resources

The websites below were accessed 1 August 2005.

ACountryLife (smallholders and downshifters):

www.acountrylife.com

Arup (Dongtan Eco-city):

www.arup.com/eastasia/project.cfm?pageid=7047

Best Foot Forward (calculating ecological footprints):

www.bestfootforward.com

BioThinking (Datschefski's ideas):

www.biothinking.com

Car clubs:

www.carplus.org.uk (Carplus)

www.citycarclub.co.uk (CityCarClub)

www.mystreetcar.co.uk (Streetcar)

www.whizzgo.co.uk (Whizzgo)

Industrial ecology:

www.cleanproduction.org (Clean Production Action)

www.mitpressjournals.org/loi/jiec (Journal of Industrial Ecology)

Interface leased carpets:

www.interfaceflooring.com/sustain

Low-energy housing:

www.bedzed.org.uk (BedZED)

www.gallionsecopark.co.uk/home.htm (Gallions Ecopark)

www.hockerton.demon.co.uk (Hockerton)

The Natural Step (sustainability for businesses):

www.naturalstep.org

Suspronet (product services):

www.suspronet.org

Acknowledgements

Grateful acknowledgement is made to the following sources for permission to reproduce material within this book.

Every effort has been made to contact copyright holders. If any have been inadvertently overlooked the publishers will be pleased to make the necessary arrangements at the first opportunity.

Text

Appendix A: Levett, R. 'A Day in the life...', *Town and Country Planning*, vol 1 Jan 2000, © Town and Country Planning Association/ Roger Levett.

Tables

Table 1: World Wide Fund for Nature (2004) *Living Planet Report*, World Wide Fund for Nature. Table 2 and 3: Worldwatch Institute (2004) *The State of Consumption*, State of the World 2004, Worldwatch Institute.

Figures

Figure 1: © Comstock Images / Alamy; Figure 2a: © John Bower / Alamy; Figure 2b: *World Urbanization Prospects: The 2003 Revision*, copyright © 2004 United Nations; Figure 3: *Changing Patterns: UK Government Framework for Sustainable Consumption and Production* (2003), DTI/DEFRA – crown copyright material is reproduced under Class Licence Number C01W0000065 with the permission of the Controller of HMSO and the Queen's Printer for Scotland; Figure 5: IKEA Ltd, © inter IKEA systems B.V. 2006; Figure 6: © Greenpeace/Natalie Behring; Figure 7: TopFoto.co.uk; Figure 8: © Bob Edwards / Science Photo Library; Figure 9: Courtesy of Interface Europe Ltd; Figure 10: © JW Luftfoto; Figure 11: Courtesy of Trek Bikes; Figure 12: Reprinted courtesy of Patagonia, Inc; Figure 13: *Changing Patterns: UK Government Framework for Sustainable Consumption and Production*, DEFRA – crown copyright material is reproduced under Class Licence Number C01W0000065 with the permission of the Controller of HMSO and the Queen's Printer for Scotland; Figure 14: *UK Energy Sector Indicators* (2005) DTI – crown copyright material is reproduced under Class Licence Number C01W0000065 with the permission of the Controller of HMSO and the Queen's Printer for Scotland; Figure 15: © David R. Frazier Photolibrary, Inc/Alamy; Figure 16: *UK Energy Sector Indicators 2005* (2005), DTI – crown copyright material is reproduced under Class Licence Number C01W0000065 with the permission of the Controller of HMSO and the Queen's Printer for Scotland; Figure 17: © Stephen Williams; Figure 18: de Beer, J. (1998) Potential for Industrial Energy Efficiency Improvement in the Long Term, University of Utrecht; Figure 19: Courtesy of Robin Roy; Figure 20: Smil V. (2003) 'Energy Linkages', *Energy at the Crossroads*, Massachusetts Institute of Technology; Figure 21a: © NRM/Science and Society Picture Library; Figure 21b: © Getty Images; Figure 21c: © EasyJet; Figure 22a and b: © Empics; Figure 22c: © Photodisc; Figure 23: Courtesy of Arup;